Grey Goo

Grey Goo

The Nano-Revolution Threat

Sam Loray

UNIEK ENTERPRISES

CONTENTS

INDEX

Chapter 7: The Role of Regulation and Policy

7.1 International efforts to regulate nanotechnology

7.2 The challenges of regulating a rapidly evolving field

7.3 The ethical and legal framework for nanotechnology research

Chapter 8: Scientists, Ethicists, and Policymakers

8.1 Perspectives from leading experts in the field

8.2 Debates and discussions on the future of nanotechnology

8.3 The importance of interdisciplinary collaboration

Chapter 9: A Call to Action

9.1 The path forward: responsible nanotechnology development

9.2 Ensuring the benefits of nanotechnology while minimizing risks

9.3 The need for public engagement, ethical considerations, and sustainable innovation

Chapter 1

Introduction to Nanotechnology

Nanotechnology, a field that has caught the creative mind of researchers and specialists the same, addresses a progressive way to deal with controlling matter at the nanoscale. The expression "nano" alludes to the size of nanometers, which is on the request for one billionth of a meter. At this scale, the way of behaving of materials wanders from the perceptible world, and novel properties arise, preparing for historic headways in different areas.

The foundations of nanotechnology can be followed back to the visionary physicist Richard Feynman, who, in his popular 1959 talk, "There's A lot of Room at the Base," featured the conceivable outcomes of controlling matter at the nuclear and sub-atomic scale. Notwithstanding, it was only after the late twentieth century that nanotechnology arose as an unmistakable logical discipline, impelled by progressions in microscopy and the combination of nanomaterials.

One of the characterizing elements of nanotechnology is its interdisciplinary nature. Drawing on standards from physical science, science, science, and designing, nanotechnology incorporates many applications and commitments groundbreaking answers for probably the most squeezing difficulties confronting humankind. As we dig further into the complexities of nanotechnology, it becomes apparent that its effect reaches out across different areas, from medication to hardware, energy, and then some.

In the domain of medication, nanotechnology holds the possibility to upset diagnostics and treatment. Nanoscale materials, for example, nanoparticles and nano-composites, can be designed to communicate with natural frameworks at the sub-atomic level. This opens up additional opportunities for designated drug conveyance, taking into consideration exact organization of therapeutics to explicit cells or tissues. Also, nanoscale gadgets can be intended for imaging and detecting, giving uncommon experiences into cell processes and empowering early discovery of infections.

In the field of gadgets, the steady quest for scaling down has prompted the advancement of nanoscale parts. Nanoelectronics use the interesting properties of materials at the nanoscale to make quicker, more modest, and more effective electronic gadgets. Quantum spots, for example, show size-subordinate electronic properties, making them promising possibility for cutting edge shows and sun powered cells. The marriage of nanotechnology and hardware is reshaping the scene of data innovation, driving advancement and introducing a period of uncommon computational power.

Energy is another space where nanotechnology is taking critical steps. The journey for reasonable and productive energy arrangements has provoked scientists to investigate nanomaterials for applications in sun oriented cells, batteries, and energy stockpiling. Nanoscale structures, for example, nanowires and nanotubes, offer upgraded surface regions and extraordinary electronic properties, working on the exhibition of energy change and capacity gadgets. Tackling the force of nanotechnology is pivotal for tending to the worldwide energy challenge and progressing towards a more maintainable future.

As we explore the many-sided trap of nanotechnology applications, it is basic to recognize the moral and cultural ramifications that go with these progressions. The capacity to control matter at the nanoscale raises worries about the potential dangers related with nanomaterials, particularly with regards to ecological effect and human wellbeing. Capable turn of events and sending of nanotechnology require an exhaustive comprehension of the expected dangers and a guarantee to moderating unfavorable impacts.

Nanotechnology's excursion from logical interest to functional applications has been set apart by surprising accomplishments and continuous difficulties. The advancement of nanomaterials with custom fitted properties has prepared for developments in regions like catalysis, detecting, and materials science. Carbon nanotubes, graphene, and quantum specks are only a couple of instances of nanomaterials that definitely stand out for their special properties and various applications.

In the domain of catalysis, nanotechnology offers new roads for planning productive and specific impetuses. The high surface region and tunable properties of nanomaterials empower exact command over synergist responses, opening up opportunities for greener and more supportable substance processes. The coordination of nanocatalysts in modern applications can possibly change the development of synthetic compounds and fills, diminishing energy utilization and natural effect.

Nanotechnology's effect on detecting innovations is similarly significant. Nanoscale sensors can recognize minute amounts of substances, making them priceless for applications in ecological checking, medical care, and security. For example, nanosensors can be utilized to distinguish explicit biomarkers characteristic of sicknesses, empowering early conclusion and customized therapy procedures. The marriage of nanotechnology and detecting is opening new elements of accuracy and responsiveness in our capacity to comprehend and cooperate with our general surroundings.

Materials science, a foundation of nanotechnology, is going through a change in outlook with the coming of nanomaterials. The control of materials at the nanoscale bestows them with special mechanical, warm, and optical properties.

This has prompted the improvement of cutting edge materials with applications going from lightweight and solid nanocomposites to shrewd materials that answer outside boosts. The plan and union of nanomaterials with custom-made properties are driving development across ventures, from aviation to development.

Chasing feasible and harmless to the ecosystem innovations, nanotechnology assumes a vital part. The plan and execution of nanomaterials for water decontamination, air filtration, and waste treatment hold guarantee for tending to squeezing ecological difficulties. Nanomaterials, for example, graphene oxide and zeolites, display remarkable adsorption properties, making them compelling for eliminating contaminations from air and water. The incorporation of nanotechnology into ecological remediation procedures highlights its true capacity as an impetus for positive change.

The convergence of nanotechnology and biotechnology opens up new wildernesses in the journey for understanding and controlling organic frameworks. Nanoscale apparatuses and gadgets give extraordinary admittance to the complexities of cell and sub-atomic cycles. Nanomedicine, a blossoming field inside nanotechnology, influences nanoscale materials for clinical applications, going from diagnostics to designated drug conveyance.

In the domain of diagnostics, nanotechnology offers imaginative answers for early illness recognition. Nanoscale imaging specialists can give high-goal pictures of natural tissues, empowering clinicians to identify irregularities at a sub-atomic level. This can possibly reform clinical diagnostics, considering early mediation and customized treatment plans. The mix of nanotechnology into clinical imaging innovations, for example, attractive reverberation imaging (X-ray) and positron discharge tomography (PET), upgrades their responsiveness and explicitness.

The field of designated drug conveyance embodies the extraordinary capability of nanotechnology in medication. Nanoparticles, liposomes, and other nanocarriers can be designed to typify restorative specialists and convey them to explicit cells or tissues. This designated approach limits the results of conventional fundamental medication organization and improves the viability of medicines. The capacity to definitively tailor drug conveyance frameworks at the nanoscale opens up additional opportunities for treating sicknesses with exceptional accuracy.

Nanotechnology's effect on regenerative medication is additionally important. The advancement of nanomaterials that copy the extracellular framework and advance tissue recovery holds guarantee for fixing harmed tissues and organs. Nanoscale platforms, cultivated with foundational microorganisms, give a helpful climate to tissue development and recovery. This combination of nanotechnology and regenerative medication can possibly reform the field of transplantation and usher in a period of regenerative treatments.

The coordination of nanotechnology into the texture of regular daily existence is turning out to be progressively apparent. Nanomaterials track down applications in customer items, going from sunscreens and materials to gadgets and food bundling. The special properties of nanomaterials, like antimicrobial movement and upgraded mechanical strength, add to the advancement of novel and further developed shopper products. Notwithstanding, this broad use brings up issues about the drawn out ecological effect of nanomaterials and the requirement for capable removal rehearses.

The appearance of nanotechnology has likewise started conversations about its expected job in the improvement of man-made consciousness (artificial intelligence). The marriage of nanotechnology and computer based intelligence holds the commitment of making smart frameworks that work at the nanoscale. Nanoscale gadgets with mental abilities could change figuring and data handling. The investigation of neuromorphic processing, roused by the design of the human mind, embodies the cooperative energies among nanotechnology and computer based intelligence.

Regardless of the wonderful advancement in nanotechnology, difficulties and vulnerabilities continue. The wellbeing of nanomaterials, both with regards to human openness and ecological effect, stays a subject of extraordinary exploration and discussion. The one of a kind properties of nanomaterials that add to their viability in different applications likewise raise worries about their possible poisonousness. Understanding the communications among nanomaterials and organic frameworks is significant for guaranteeing the protected and dependable improvement of nanotechnology.

1.1 The promise and potential of nanotechnology

Nanotechnology, with its underlying foundations in the control of issue at the nanoscale, holds a commitment that reverberates across logical, mechanical, and cultural scenes. This blossoming field has arisen as an impetus for development, offering unmatched potential to change different areas and address probably the most squeezing difficulties confronting humankind. At the core of nanotechnology is the capacity to design materials and gadgets at aspects on the request for nanometers, opening novel properties and functionalities that contrast generally from those at bigger scopes.

One of the characterizing highlights of nanotechnology is its interdisciplinary nature. Drawing on standards from material science, science, science, and designing, nanotechnology traverses a range of uses, from medication and gadgets to energy and ecological remediation. The intermingling of these different disciplines has made a fruitful ground for investigation, prompting momentous progressions that were once bound to the domains of sci-fi.

In the domain of medication, nanotechnology has introduced another period of potential outcomes. The capacity to control matter at the nanoscale has made ready for advancements in diagnostics, drug conveyance, and regenerative medication.

Nanoparticles, nanosensors, and nanodevices are at the very front of these progressions, offering extraordinary accuracy in the comprehension and treatment of sicknesses.

Nanotechnology's effect on diagnostics is especially imperative. Nanoscale imaging specialists and sensors give a degree of detail that was once incredible. These devices empower clinicians to identify irregularities at a sub-atomic level, working with early finding and customized treatment methodologies. The reconciliation of nanotechnology into clinical imaging advancements improves their responsiveness and particularity, promising a change in perspective by they way we approach illness location and checking.

In the domain of medication conveyance, nanotechnology offers a designated and effective methodology. Nanoparticles and nanocarriers can be designed to typify restorative specialists and convey them to explicit cells or tissues. This designated conveyance limits the secondary effects related with customary fundamental organization and improves the viability of medicines. The marriage of nanotechnology and medication conveyance is changing the scene of medication, giving new roads to treating illnesses with phenomenal accuracy.

Regenerative medication, one more wilderness inside nanotechnology, investigates the capability of nanomaterials to advance tissue recovery and fix. Nanoscale platforms, frequently cultivated with immature microorganisms, establish a climate helpful for tissue development. This combination of nanotechnology and regenerative medication holds guarantee for tending to difficulties in transplantation and introducing another time of regenerative treatments.

The effect of nanotechnology isn't restricted to the domain of medication; it reaches out to the center of gadgets and data innovation. The persevering quest for scaling down has prompted the improvement of nanoelectronics, where nanoscale parts show special electronic properties. Quantum specks, graphene, and nanowires are only a couple of instances of nanomaterials that are reshaping the scene of electronic gadgets.

Nanoelectronics isn't simply about making gadgets more modest; it is tied in with utilizing the unmistakable properties of materials at the nanoscale. Quantum specks, for example, show size-subordinate electronic way of behaving, making them promising possibility for applications, for example, cutting edge shows and sunlight based cells. The coordination of nanotechnology into gadgets is driving development, pushing the limits of what is conceivable concerning computational power, energy productivity, and gadget usefulness.

Energy, a basic worldwide test, is likewise a space where nanotechnology is exhibiting huge potential. The plan and execution of nanomaterials for energy transformation and capacity are at the very front of supportable energy arrangements. Nanoscale structures, including nanowires and nanotubes, offer upgraded surface regions and extraordinary electronic properties, working on the productivity of gadgets like sun based cells and batteries.

The mission for effective and practical energy arrangements has provoked analysts to investigate nanomaterials for their likely in outfitting and putting away energy. Nanotechnology holds the way to tending to the consistently developing interest for energy while limiting natural effect. The improvement of nanomaterials for energy applications embodies the extraordinary capability of nanotechnology in molding a more practical future.

Natural remediation is another field where nanotechnology shows tending to worldwide challenges potential. The interesting properties of nanomaterials make them compelling instruments for water sanitization, air filtration, and waste treatment. Nanomaterials, for example, graphene oxide and zeolites, display excellent adsorption properties, giving imaginative answers for eliminating toxins from the climate.

The reconciliation of nanotechnology into natural remediation methodologies highlights its job as an impetus for positive change. As the world wrestles with issues of water shortage, air contamination, and waste administration, nanotechnology offers a tool compartment of accuracy and proficiency. The capacity to tailor nanomaterials for explicit ecological difficulties holds guarantee for making manageable arrangements that line up with the standards of roundabout and green innovations.

In spite of the momentous commitment of nanotechnology, its excursion from logical interest to reasonable application isn't without difficulties and contemplations. One of the first worries is the security of nanomaterials, both regarding human openness and natural effect. The special properties that make nanomaterials viable in different applications likewise bring up issues about their expected harmfulness.

Understanding the associations among nanomaterials and natural frameworks is essential for guaranteeing the protected and capable advancement of nanotechnology. Analysts are effectively researching the potential dangers related with nanomaterials, intending to lay out rules and conventions that moderate unfriendly impacts. Moral contemplations encompassing the sending of nanotechnology stretch out past well-being worries to incorporate issues of value, access, and cultural ramifications.

The impartial sending of nanotechnology is a basic thought as its applications keep on multiplying. Inquiries regarding admittance to nanotechnology and its advantages, especially with regards to worldwide incongruities, feature the requirement for an insightful and comprehensive methodology. As nanotechnology turns out to be progressively coordinated into customer items and daily existence, tending to these moral contemplations becomes vital.

The cultural ramifications of nanotechnology stretch out to reshaping economies and industries potential. The production of new business sectors, the change of existing enterprises, and the development of completely clever applications highlight the broad effect of nanotechnology on cultural designs. Exploring these progressions requires a proactive and comprehensive methodology that thinks about the interests and prosperity of different partners.

The crossing point of nanotechnology and man-made consciousness (computer based intelligence) adds one more layer to the unfurling story. The mix of nanoscale gadgets with mental abilities holds the commitment of making astute frameworks that work at extraordinary scales. Neuromorphic figuring, enlivened by the engineering of the human cerebrum, epitomizes the collaborations among nanotechnology and artificial intelligence.

The potential for nanotechnology to add to the improvement of canny frameworks brings up issues about the moral ramifications of these advancements. As we investigate the intermingling of nanotechnology and artificial intelligence, it is fundamental to think about issues of security, independence, and the cultural effect of canny frameworks working at the nanoscale. Moral systems and administration structures should develop close by innovative progressions to guarantee capable turn of events and arrangement.

With regards to nanotechnology's commitment and potential, it is vital for encourage a culture of interest, joint effort, and moral reflection. The excursion into the nanoscale domain isn't just a logical and innovative experience yet in addition a cultural and moral endeavor. As nanotechnology keeps on developing, it is pivotal to move toward its improvement with an all encompassing viewpoint, taking into account the specialized progressions as well as the moral, cultural, and ecological ramifications.

The commitment of nanotechnology lies not simply in that frame of mind to make novel materials and gadgets yet in its capability to address a portion of the fabulous difficulties confronting mankind. From propelling clinical medicines to changing gadgets and adding to maintainable energy arrangements, nanotechnology is an extraordinary power that requests mindful stewardship.

As we stand at the convergence of logical revelation and mechanical advancement, it is occupant upon society to explore the commitments and possibilities of nanotechnology with prescience and intelligence. This involves cultivating a unique discourse between researchers, policymakers, ethicists, and the general population to shape the direction of nanotechnology in a way that lines up with our aggregate qualities and goals. The commitment of nanotechnology isn't simply a brief look into the future; it is a challenge to effectively participate in molding a future where the capability of nanotechnology is bridled to support all.

1.2 Nanoscale properties and applications

The properties of materials at the nanoscale address a captivating domain where regular principles of physical science and science go through groundbreaking movements. As we dive into the complexities of nanoscale properties, it becomes obvious that peculiarities at this level are unmistakably unique in relation to those saw at bigger scopes. Nanotechnology, which includes the control and use of issue at aspects commonly going from 1 to 100 nanometers, investigates and takes advantage of these special properties for a horde of utilizations across different disciplines.

One of the central parts of nanoscale properties is the expanded surface region to-volume proportion displayed by nanomaterials. As the size of particles diminishes, the relative surface region accessible for connections with the general climate turns out to be more critical. This peculiarity grants nanomaterials with improved reactivity, making them especially important in catalysis and synthetic detecting applications. The expanded surface region takes into consideration more proficient associations among nanomaterials and different substances, impacting their compound and actual ways of behaving.

Quantum impacts, one more unmistakable component of nanoscale properties, become possibly the most important factor as the size of materials moves toward the quantum scale. At this level, the way of behaving of particles is administered by quantum mechanics, prompting peculiarities, for example, quantum restriction and quantum burrowing. Quantum specks, for example, are nanoscale semiconductor particles that display size-subordinate electronic and optical properties because of quantum repression. These properties make quantum specks promising possibility for applications in gadgets, photonics, and clinical imaging.

The optical properties of nanomaterials, frequently connected with their size and shape, add to their extraordinary qualities. Nanoparticles can show colors that are re-liant upon their size and sythesis, a peculiarity known as plasmon reverberation. This property is bridled in different applications, including biosensing and imaging. The tunability of plasmon reverberation in nanomaterials considers the improvement of sensors that can identify explicit biomolecules with high responsiveness.

Attractive properties at the nanoscale present novel open doors for applications in information capacity, clinical imaging, and attractive reverberation imaging (X-ray). Attractive nanoparticles, for example, iron oxide nanoparticles, can be controlled uti-lizing outer attractive fields, empowering designated drug conveyance in medication or upgrading contrast in imaging methods. The command over attractive properties at the nanoscale opens roads for the advancement of inventive innovations with critical cultural effect.

Electrical conductivity at the nanoscale is an essential property that underlies progressions in nanoelectronics. Nanomaterials, like carbon nanotubes and graphene, display outstanding electrical conductivity because of their special electronic designs. This has prompted the investigation of these materials in the improvement of elite execution electronic gadgets. The reconciliation of nanoscale materials in hardware is driving the scaling down of parts, upgrading gadget execution, and preparing for the up and coming age of registering advancements.

Mechanical properties at the nanoscale challenge how we might interpret material way of behaving. Nanomaterials frequently show outstanding mechanical strength and adaptability, and these properties find applications in regions like materials science and nanomechanical gadgets. Carbon nanotubes, for example, are famous for their amazing strength, lightweight nature, and adaptability, making them ideal possibility for the improvement of cutting edge materials with applications in aviation and primary designing.

The warm properties of nanomaterials, including warm conductivity and strength, are pivotal contemplations in fields, for example, nanoelectronics and materials science. Nanoscale structures, for example, nanowires and nanotubes, display extraordinary warm conductivities that vary from their mass partners. Understanding and controlling warm properties at the nanoscale are fundamental for planning materials with customized qualities for explicit applications, from thermoelectric gadgets to warm administration in hardware.

The multi-layered nature of nanoscale properties considers their application in assorted fields, adding to mechanical headways and cultural advantages. In medication, nanoscale properties are saddled for the improvement of nanomedicines and demonstrative apparatuses. Nanoparticles can be intended to collaborate specifically with natural particles, empowering designated drug conveyance and imaging with accuracy at the phone and sub-atomic levels. The improved surface region and reactivity of nanomaterials assume a urgent part in the viability of these applications.

In hardware, the abuse of nanoscale properties is driving the advancement of quicker, more modest, and more effective gadgets. Nanomaterials with uncommon electrical conductivity, for example, graphene, are upsetting the field of nanoelectronics. The scaling down of parts and the investigation of quantum impacts at the nanoscale are molding the eventual fate of data innovation, with suggestions for processing power, correspondence, and information stockpiling.

Energy applications benefit altogether from the one of a kind properties of nanomaterials. Nanotechnology assumes a crucial part in the improvement of cutting edge materials for sun powered cells, batteries, and energy stockpiling gadgets. Nanoscale structures, for example, nanowires and quantum dabs, improve the productivity of energy transformation and capacity processes. The plan and designing of nanomaterials for energy applications add to the mission for feasible and environmentally friendly power arrangements.

Ecological remediation is another area where nanoscale properties track down viable applications. Nanomaterials with extraordinary adsorption and reactant properties can be utilized for the expulsion of contaminations from air and water. The high surface region and reactivity of nanomaterials improve their adequacy in catching and corrupting pollutants. This crossing point of nanotechnology and natural science holds guarantee for addressing difficulties connected with water refinement, air quality, and waste treatment.

The coordination of nanoscale properties into ordinary items is turning out to be progressively common. Nanomaterials track down applications in customer products, materials, and coatings, adding to the advancement of novel and further developed materials. The antimicrobial properties of certain nanomaterials make them important increases to items, for example, food bundling and clinical gadgets, upgrading cleanliness and wellbeing.

In spite of the striking capability of nanoscale properties, moving toward their applications with a careful thought of expected chances and moral implications is essential. The wellbeing of nanomaterials, both concerning human openness and natural effect, stays a subject of continuous examination and administrative investigation. Capable turn of events and organization of nanotechnology require an extensive comprehension of the expected dangers and a guarantee to relieving unfavorable impacts.

As we investigate the commitment and capability of nanoscale properties, it is fundamental to perceive the interconnectedness of logical, innovative, and cultural aspects. The union of disciplines in nanotechnology epitomizes the requirement for cooperative and interdisciplinary ways to deal with address complex difficulties. Moral contemplations, including issues of security, value, and cultural ramifications, should be coordinated into the texture of nanotechnology improvement to guarantee its capable and manageable progression.

1.3 Historical perspective on nanotechnology's growth

The verifiable direction of nanotechnology's development is a story that unfurls at the crossing point of logical interest, mechanical advancement, and the quest for understanding and controlling matter at the nanoscale. While the expression "nanotechnology" itself acquired noticeable quality in the last 50% of the twentieth 100 years, its foundations can be followed back to early logical requests and mechanical advancements that established the groundwork for the development of this progressive field.

The preface to nanotechnology can be tracked down underway of spearheading researchers who, in the mid twentieth hundred years, dug into the domains of quantum mechanics and nuclear physical science. Richard Feynman's well known 1959 talk, "There's A lot of Room at the Base," is in many cases considered an impetus for conceptualizing the conceivable outcomes of controlling matter at the nuclear and sub-atomic scale. Feynman's vision set up for the investigation of the nanoscale world, despite the fact that the expression "nanotechnology" had not yet been instituted.

The 1980s saw an essential second with the coming of checking burrowing microscopy (STM) and nuclear power microscopy (AFM). These weighty imaging procedures, created by Gerd Binnig and Heinrich Rohrer, permitted researchers to envision and control individual molecules with uncommon accuracy. The capacity to "see" and connect with issue at the nanoscale opened new roads for logical request and mechanical progressions, laying the foundation for the formalization of nanotechnology as an unmistakable field.

The expression "nanotechnology" was promoted by the Nobel laureate Eric Drexler during the 1980s through his persuasive book "Motors of Creation." Drexler's work imagined the development of nanoscale machines and gadgets through a cycle he named "sub-atomic assembling."

While Drexler's vision ignited both energy and wariness, it assumed an essential part in carrying nanotechnology into the public cognizance and animating further logical investigation.

The proper foundation of nanotechnology as a logical discipline picked up speed during the 1990s, set apart by the send off of the Public Nanotechnology Drive (NNI) in the US in 2000. The NNI, a multi-organization drive, meant to facilitate and subsidize research in nanoscience and nanotechnology across different areas. This noticeable a coordinated work to use nanotechnology for financial development and address cultural difficulties.

The development of nanotechnology was not restricted to the US. All over the planet, research organizations, colleges, and businesses started to put resources into nanoscience and nanotechnology. States perceived the groundbreaking capability of nanotechnology and started financing projects to help innovative work in this prospering field. The cooperative and interdisciplinary nature of nanotechnology turned out to be progressively clear as scientists from different foundations added to its development.

In the beginning phases, nanotechnology research principally centered around major science and understanding the properties of materials at the nanoscale. As the field developed, consideration moved toward pragmatic applications across different areas. Nanomaterials, with their exceptional properties, arose as key parts for developments in medication, gadgets, energy, and materials science.

The field of nanomedicine saw huge development, with analysts investigating the utilization of nanoscale materials for clinical diagnostics, drug conveyance, and imaging. Nanoparticles could be designed to target explicit cells or tissues, reforming the accuracy of medication conveyance and decreasing aftereffects. Nanoscale imaging specialists took into account high-goal imaging at the sub-atomic level, upgrading indicative abilities and empowering early identification of illnesses.

In hardware, the scaling down of parts turned into a main thrust behind the development of nanotechnology. Nanoscale materials, like carbon nanotubes and graphene, displayed novel electrical properties that made ready for the improvement of quicker and more effective electronic gadgets. Nanoelectronics turned into a point of convergence of examination, with suggestions for data innovation, correspondence, and the semiconductor business.

Energy utilizations of nanotechnology acquired conspicuousness as scientists investigated nanomaterials for sun oriented cells, batteries, and energy stockpiling. The plan and designing of nanoscale structures added to upgrades in energy change and capacity effectiveness. Nanotechnology assumed an essential part in progressing manageable and environmentally friendly power arrangements, lining up with worldwide endeavors to address the difficulties of energy security and ecological supportability.

The natural and reactant utilizations of nanotechnology likewise arose as critical areas of development. Nanomaterials were used for water refinement, air filtration, and waste treatment. The high surface region and reactivity of nanomaterials made them viable in catching and corrupting poisons. The assembly of nanotechnology and natural science opened additional opportunities for resolving major problems connected with water quality, air contamination, and waste administration.

The commercialization of nanotechnology applications picked up speed in the 21st hundred years. Ventures started consolidating nanomaterials into shopper items, going from hardware and materials to food bundling and beauty care products. The exceptional properties of nanomaterials, like antimicrobial movement and upgraded mechanical strength, added to the advancement of novel and further developed materials.

The interdisciplinary idea of nanotechnology turned out to be progressively obvious as joint efforts between researchers, designers, and industry specialists prospered. The union of aptitude from physical science, science, science, and designing was fundamental for the advancement of creative nanotechnologies. The joining of information across disciplines was a main thrust behind the flexibility and extraordinary capability of nanotechnology.

Notwithstanding the astounding development and potential, nanotechnology confronted difficulties and moral contemplations. Worries about the wellbeing of nanomaterials, both concerning human openness and natural effect, incited continuous exploration and administrative investigation. The extraordinary properties that made nanomaterials viable additionally brought up issues about their possible harmfulness. Moral contemplations stretched out past wellbeing worries to include issues of value, access, and cultural ramifications, featuring the requirement for capable turn of events and sending.

As nanotechnology kept on developing, worldwide coordinated effort turned out to be progressively significant. The sharing of information, assets, and best practices worked with progress in nanoscience and nanotechnology on a worldwide scale. Associations like the Worldwide Nanotechnology Meeting on Correspondence and Participation (INC) assumed a urgent part in cultivating coordinated effort and propelling the dependable improvement of nanotechnology.

Looking toward the future, the development of nanotechnology holds the commitment of proceeded with advancement and groundbreaking arrangements. The union of nanotechnology with other arising fields, like computerized reasoning and biotechnology, opens new wildernesses for investigation. The mix of nanoscale gadgets with mental capacities and the investigation of bio-nano interfaces epitomize the collaborations that could shape the following period of nanotechnology's development.

Chapter 2

The Nano-Revolution Unveiled

The Nano-Upset, an epochal change in our comprehension and control of issue at the nanoscale, has divulged a groundbreaking period where the littlest aspects yield the main effects. This upset, established in the combination of different logical disciplines, mechanical developments, and a significant comprehension of materials at the nuclear and sub-atomic levels, has introduced a change in outlook with broad ramifications across assorted areas.

At the core of the Nano-Insurgency lies the interdisciplinary idea of nano-technology. Drawing bits of knowledge from physical science, science, science, and designing, this field embodies the control of materials at aspects on the request for one billionth of a meter. The investigation of the nanoscale, a space that obscures the limits between traditional physical science and quantum mechanics, has turned into a cauldron for development and an impetus for headways that were once the domain of creative mind.

By and large, the excursion toward the Nano-Upset can be followed back to the mid twentieth 100 years, when trailblazers in quantum mechanics and nuclear physical science laid the hypothetical basis. Notwithstanding, it was only after the last 50% of the century that nanotechnology arose as a particular field, driven by the visionary thoughts of researchers like Richard Feynman. His 1959 talk, "There's A lot of Room at the Base," ignited the creative mind of scientists and made way for the investigation of the nanoscale world.

The defining moment accompanied the improvement of progressive imaging procedures during the 1980s - checking burrowing microscopy (STM) and nuclear power microscopy (AFM). These forward leaps, spearheaded by Gerd Binnig and Heinrich Rohrer, gave the initial looks into the nanoscale domain, permitting researchers to envision and control individual iotas with uncommon accuracy. The capacity to notice and connect with issue at such a key level denoted the origin of the Nano-Upset.

The formalization of nanotechnology as a field picked up speed during the 1990s and finished in the send off of the Public Nanotechnology Drive (NNI) in the US in

2000. The NNI, a cooperative exertion across different government offices, meant to facilitate and support research in nanoscience and nanotechnology. This noticeable a vital second, as it flagged the acknowledgment of nanotechnology's capability to drive financial development, prod mechanical advancement, and address squeezing cultural difficulties.

As nanotechnology developed, specialists dug into the principal properties of materials at the nanoscale. The expanded surface region to-volume proportion arose as a central trademark, impacting the reactivity and properties of nanomaterials.

Quantum impacts, a result of working at the quantum scale, presented new peculiarities, testing how we might interpret materials and opening roads for extraordinary applications.

Quantum dabs, for instance, embody the effect of quantum impacts. These nanoscale semiconductor particles show size-subordinate electronic and optical properties because of quantum restriction. The tunability of quantum specks has tracked down applications in gadgets, photonics, and clinical imaging, displaying the extraordinary capability of nanotechnology in different areas.

Nanotechnology's effect on medication has been significant, prompting the development of nanomedicine as a particular field. The capacity to control matter at the nanoscale has worked with developments in diagnostics, drug conveyance, and regenerative medication. Nanoparticles, with their custom fitted properties, can be designed to collaborate specifically with natural substances, offering remarkable accuracy in clinical applications.

In diagnostics, nanotechnology has empowered the improvement of high-goal imaging specialists and sensors. Nanoscale devices give experiences into cell and atomic cycles, working with early location of infections. The accuracy managed by nanoscale imaging upgrades symptomatic capacities, promising a change in outlook in clinical diagnostics.

Drug conveyance, a foundation of nanomedicine, influences nanoscale transporters to move restorative specialists to explicit cells or tissues. Nanoparticles, liposomes, and other nanocarriers safeguard drugs from debasement, improve their dissolvability, and empower designated conveyance. This designated approach limits secondary effects and works on the viability of medicines, proclaiming another time in customized medication.

Regenerative medication, a boondocks inside nanotechnology, investigates the capability of nanomaterials to advance tissue recovery. Nanoscale frameworks, frequently cultivated with immature microorganisms, establish a helpful climate for tissue development. This union of nanotechnology and regenerative medication holds guarantee for fixing harmed tissues and organs, introducing groundbreaking opportunities for transplantation and regenerative treatments.

Hardware, one more stronghold of nanotechnology, has seen an upheaval in the scaling down of parts and the investigation of nanoscale materials. Carbon nanotubes and graphene, with their phenomenal electrical conductivity, have become leaders in the advancement of nanoelectronics. The coordination of nanoscale materials has pushed headways in data innovation, correspondence, and gadget usefulness.

The exceptional properties of nanoscale materials, especially their electrical conductivity, have re-imagined the scene of gadgets. Carbon nanotubes, barrel shaped designs of carbon molecules, show uncommon electrical and warm conductivity.

Graphene, a solitary layer of carbon particles organized in a hexagonal grid, has surprising electrical, warm, and mechanical properties. These materials are at the front of exploration pointed toward growing superior execution electronic gadgets.

The mission for energy arrangements, interweaved with the worldwide test of manageability, has seen nanotechnology assume a urgent part. Nanomaterials have been saddled in sunlight based cells, batteries, and energy stockpiling gadgets to improve effectiveness and execution. Nanoscale structures, for example, nanowires and quantum spots, advance energy transformation processes and add to the improvement of maintainable energy innovations.

In sunlight based cells, nanotechnology has worked with the plan of cutting edge materials with worked on light assimilation and charge transport properties. Nanomaterials, for example, quantum specks, show size-subordinate electronic properties that upgrade their effectiveness in changing over daylight into power. The mix of nanotechnology into sunlight based energy applications holds guarantee for tending to the developing interest for spotless and sustainable power sources.

Energy capacity advancements, including batteries and supercapacitors, benefit from nanotechnology's impact on materials. Nanoscale anodes and nanocomposite materials upgrade the exhibition of energy stockpiling gadgets, prompting progressions in electric vehicles, compact hardware, and framework stockpiling. The capacity to fit materials at the nanoscale adds to the advancement of lightweight, high-limit energy capacity arrangements.

Natural remediation, a basic notwithstanding raising ecological difficulties, has tracked down a partner in nanotechnology. Nanomaterials, with their interesting adsorption and reactant properties, offer creative answers for water decontamination, air filtration, and waste treatment. The high surface region and reactivity of nanomaterials make them successful apparatuses for catching and debasing poisons, resolving issues connected with water quality, air contamination, and waste administration.

The convergence of nanotechnology and natural science highlights the field's capability to add to supportable arrangements. Nanomaterials, for example, graphene oxide and zeolites have shown remarkable adsorption capacities, making them significant in eliminating pollutants from water sources. The exact designing of nanomaterials considers designated approaches in natural remediation, lining up with the standards of green and round advances.

The reconciliation of nanotechnology into purchaser items and regular daily existence is meaningful of its boundless effect. Nanomaterials track down applications in materials, coatings, gadgets, and food bundling, adding to the advancement of novel and further developed materials. Antimicrobial properties of certain nanomaterials upgrade the wellbeing of items, while the mechanical strength of nanocomposites works on the sturdiness and execution of materials.

Regardless of the extraordinary capability of nanotechnology, challenges and moral contemplations go with its development. Wellbeing concerns in regards to the possible poisonousness of nanomaterials, both for human openness and natural effect, require progressing research and administrative oversight. The extraordinary properties that make nanomaterials powerful likewise bring up issues about their drawn out impacts, provoking a careful way to deal with their organization.

Moral contemplations reach out past wellbeing worries to envelop issues of value, access, and cultural ramifications. As nanotechnology turns out to be progressively co-ordinated into different areas, questions emerge about who benefits from these head-ways and whether there are potentially negative side-effects that lopsidedly influence specific populaces. Tending to these moral contemplations is pivotal for guaranteeing the mindful and fair advancement of nanotechnology.

The combination of nanotechnology with man-made brainpower (computer based intelligence) acquaints new aspects with the Nano-Unrest. The reconciliation of nanoscale gadgets with mental abilities, known as neuromorphic processing, holds the commitment of making clever frameworks that work at uncommon scales. The collaboration among nanotechnology and computer based intelligence represents the unique idea of innovative intermingling .

2.1 Advancements in nanotechnology research

Headways in nanotechnology research have moved this interdisciplinary field to the front line of logical and mechanical development, offering a huge number of con-ceivable outcomes that reach out across different spaces. From medication to gadgets, energy to materials science, nanotechnology has turned into a main thrust in forming the direction of mechanical advancement. This story digs into key headways, featuring the extraordinary effect of nanotechnology research on different areas and framing the expected future bearings of this unique field.

In the domain of medication, nanotechnology has seen noteworthy steps, in a gen-eral sense changing the scene of diagnostics, drug conveyance, and helpful mediations. One essential area of progress is in the advancement of nanoscale imaging specialists for clinical diagnostics. Nanoparticles, for example, quantum specks and attractive nanoparticles, offer exceptional properties that improve imaging modalities like attrac-tive reverberation imaging (X-ray) and fluorescence imaging. The accuracy managed by these nanoscale specialists considers the recognition of irregularities at the sub-atomic level, working with early conclusion and customized treatment procedures.

In the field of diagnostics, nanotechnology has given creative devices to recognizing biomarkers related with illnesses. Nanosensors, frequently founded on standards of surface plasmon reverberation or quantum dabs, empower profoundly delicate and explicit discovery of natural particles.

These nanoscale gadgets have applications in reason behind care diagnostics, offering fast and precise evaluations that can illuminate convenient clinical choices. The marriage of nanotechnology with diagnostics embodies its capability to upset medical services by giving prior and more exact recognition of infections.

The excursion into nanomedicine stretches out to progressions in drug conveyance, where nanotechnology has acquainted groundbreaking methodologies with upgrade the adequacy and decrease the symptoms of helpful specialists. Nanoparticles, liposomes, and dendrimers act as transporters for drugs, taking into account designated conveyance to explicit cells or tissues. This designated approach limits harm to sound tissues, defeating impediments related with regular fundamental medication organization. The capacity to design nanocarriers with controlled discharge properties further refines drug conveyance techniques, streamlining helpful results.

Also, nanotechnology has prodded headways in regenerative medication, offering answers for tissue designing and fix. Nanomaterials, like nanofibers and nanoparticles, give frameworks that emulate the extracellular lattice, establishing a climate helpful for tissue development. The joining of nanotechnology with regenerative medication holds guarantee for tending to difficulties in organ transplantation and tissue fix, encouraging the improvement of novel treatments with the possibility to reform the field.

In the space of hardware, nanotechnology has catalyzed an upheaval in scaling down and the improvement of nanoelectronic gadgets. The investigation of nanoscale materials, like carbon nanotubes and graphene, has made ready for progressions in nanoelectronics. Carbon nanotubes, with their striking electrical conductivity and mechanical strength, have been investigated for applications in semiconductors and interconnects. Essentially, graphene, a solitary layer of carbon molecules, shows special electronic properties that make it an alluring possibility for cutting edge electronic gadgets.

The joining of nanoscale materials has prompted progressions in customary hardware as well as brought about the field of quantum figuring. Quantum spots, which are semiconductor nanoparticles, are at the very front of quantum registering research. Their size-subordinate electronic properties and quantum repression impacts make them promising contender for qubits — the fundamental units of quantum data. Quantum spots, alongside other nanoscale parts, add to the advancement of quantum PCs that hold the possibility to outflank traditional PCs in unambiguous computational errands.

Energy applications have seen critical headways driven by nanotechnology research, especially in the improvement of nanomaterials for sun powered cells and energy stockpiling gadgets. Nanoscale structures, for example, quantum spots and nanowires, upgrade the proficiency of sun oriented cells by working on light retention and charge transport.

The capacity to design nanomaterials for ideal energy change has suggestions for the advancement of productive and practical sunlight based energy innovations.

In the domain of energy stockpiling, nanotechnology plays had an essential impact in propelling batteries and supercapacitors. Nanomaterials, including nanotubes and nanocomposite materials, add to the improvement of energy stockpiling gadgets' exhibition. The high surface region and exceptional properties of nanomaterials empower quicker charge-release cycles and higher energy densities, tending to difficulties related with the energy stockpiling requests of current advances.

Ecological remediation has arisen as a key region where nanotechnology offers creative answers for address contamination and natural difficulties. Nanomaterials, for example, nanoparticles and nanocomposites, display striking adsorption and synergist properties that can be bridled for water purging and air filtration. Nanoparticles can be intended to catch poisons, and reactant nanoparticles can work with the debasement of impurities, giving supportable and effective answers for ecological cleanup.

The assembly of nanotechnology with ecological science reaches out to the improvement of nanomaterials for water treatment. Graphene oxide, for instance, has shown remarkable adsorption capacities for many contaminations, including weighty metals and natural mixtures. The high surface region and tunable properties of graphene oxide make it a flexible material for water cleansing innovations, offering an expected solution for water shortage and contamination.

Progressions in materials science driven by nanotechnology research have prompted the making of novel materials with upgraded properties. Nanocomposites, which consolidate nanomaterials into customary networks, show unrivaled mechanical, warm, and electrical properties. The support of materials with nanoscale parts has applications in aviation, car, and development ventures, adding to the improvement of lightweight and superior execution materials.

The coordination of nanotechnology into shopper items highlights its effect on regular daily existence. Nanomaterials track down applications in coatings, materials, and hardware, improving the usefulness and execution of a heap of items. Hostile to intelligent coatings in light of nanotechnology work on the lucidity of eyeglasses and camera focal points, while nanoparticle-based sunscreens give better assurance against hurtful bright beams. The antimicrobial properties of certain nanomaterials make them significant augmentations to buyer products, adding to further developed cleanliness and wellbeing.

As nanotechnology keeps on propelling, the convergence of nanotechnology with other arising fields, like computerized reasoning (artificial intelligence), holds the commitment of groundbreaking collaborations.

The incorporation of nanoscale gadgets with mental abilities, known as neuromorphic figuring, epitomizes the likely intermingling of nanotechnology and computer based intelligence. Neuromorphic registering draws motivation from the engineering of the human mind, planning to make insightful frameworks that work at uncommon scales.

The possible utilizations of neuromorphic registering reach out to regions, for example, design acknowledgment, AI, and mental processing. The mix of nanoscale gadgets with mental functionalities addresses a wilderness in registering, with suggestions for the improvement of clever frameworks that can perform complex undertakings with effectiveness and flexibility. The cooperative energies among nanotechnology and simulated intelligence embody the powerful idea of mechanical union and reshaping enterprises and societies potential.

Looking forward, the direction of nanotechnology research highlights considerably bigger potentials and difficulties. The proceeded with investigation of the nanoscale domain will probably yield new materials, gadgets, and applications that push the limits of what is mechanically practical. The coordination of nanotechnology with other arising fields, combined with continuous endeavors to comprehend and moderate likely dangers, will shape the mindful turn of events and arrangement of nanotechnology later on.

Be that as it may, as nanotechnology keeps on developing, tending to difficulties and moral considerations is basic. Wellbeing concerns encompassing the expected harmfulness of nanomaterials, both for human openness and natural effect, require progressing research and administrative examination. Moral contemplations stretch out past security worries to envelop issues of value, access, and cultural ramifications. The capable turn of events and organization of nanotechnology require a far reaching comprehension of possible dangers and a pledge to moderating unfavorable impacts.

All in all, the headways in nanotechnology research have introduced an extraordinary time set apart by logical revelation, mechanical development, and the combination of different disciplines. From the accuracy of nanoscale imaging specialists in medication to the effectiveness of nanomaterials in energy applications, nanotechnology has turned into an unyielding power forming the fate of innovation. As we explore the intricacies of nanotechnology's development, it is basic to move toward its improvement with a comprehensive viewpoint, taking into account logical progressions close by moral.

2.2 Emerging breakthroughs in medicine, materials science, and more

The scene of logical and mechanical forward leaps is continually advancing, with new disclosures reshaping how we might interpret the world and pushing the limits of advancement. As of late, a few arising leap forwards stand out across different disciplines, offering groundbreaking prospects in medication, materials science, and then some. This story investigates a portion of these forward leaps, digging into the potential effect they might have on the manner in which we approach medical care, make progressed materials, and address squeezing worldwide difficulties.

Medication: Reforming Medical services through Nanomedicine

One of the most encouraging and quickly propelling fields inside medication is nanomedicine, where the control of materials at the nanoscale is bridled to reform diagnostics, drug conveyance, and helpful mediations. Nanoparticles, with their special properties, act as adaptable apparatuses in this undertaking.

In diagnostics, nanotechnology has opened up new wildernesses with the improvement of profoundly touchy and explicit nanosensors. These sensors can recognize biomarkers related with different sicknesses at the sub-atomic level, empowering early and exact finding. Nanoscale imaging specialists, for example, quantum spots and attractive nanoparticles, have improved clinical imaging modalities, furnishing clinicians with uncommon bits of knowledge into cell and sub-atomic cycles.

The use of nanotechnology in drug conveyance has been a unique advantage in customized medication. Nanoparticles and nanocarriers can be designed to convey helpful specialists with accuracy to explicit cells or tissues, limiting incidental effects and further developing treatment viability. This designated drug conveyance approach can possibly change the scene of disease therapy, where the test lies in specifically focusing on malignant growth cells while saving solid tissues.

Additionally, nanotechnology has prodded advancements in regenerative medication, offering answers for tissue designing and organ transplantation. Nanomaterials, like nanofibers and frameworks, give a helpful climate to tissue development and recovery. This crossing point of nanotechnology with regenerative medication holds guarantee for tending to the basic deficiency of benefactor organs and propelling the field of transplantation.

Past these applications, the assembly of nanotechnology and medication has brought about the advancement of theranostic stages, which join demonstrative and helpful functionalities. Nanoparticles can be intended to all the while convey sedates and give continuous imaging of the treatment's adequacy. This incorporated methodology holds extraordinary potential for fitting medicines to individual patients, streamlining restorative results, and diminishing the general weight of infection.

Materials Science: Designing the Future with Nanomaterials

Materials science remains at the front of various leap forwards, determined by the capacity to design materials at the nanoscale. Nanomaterials, portrayed by their exceptional properties, have opened new roads for making progressed materials with applications going from gadgets to energy capacity.

In the domain of hardware, nanotechnology has empowered the improvement of nanoelectronic gadgets that stretch the boundaries of scaling down. Carbon-based nanomaterials, for example, graphene and carbon nanotubes, display excellent electrical conductivity and mechanical strength.

Analysts are investigating their utilization in semiconductors, interconnects, and different parts, with the possibility to upset the gadgets business by making quicker, more modest, and more energy-proficient gadgets.

Quantum figuring, an area of extreme examination and investigation, is one more boondocks in materials science. Nanoscale parts, for example, quantum dabs, are being explored for their quantum processing potential. These little semiconductor particles can work as qubits, the fundamental units of quantum data. The marriage of nanotechnology with quantum registering holds the commitment of computational capacities that outperform old style PCs in tackling complex issues.

Energy applications have benefited essentially from progressions in nanomaterials. In sun oriented energy, nanotechnology plays had a vital impact in working on the productivity of sun powered cells. Nanoscale structures, for example, quantum spots and nanowires, upgrade light ingestion and charge transport, adding to the advancement of more productive and savvy sun based energy innovations.

Nanotechnology has additionally made huge commitments to energy capacity, tending to the developing interest for superior execution batteries and supercapacitors. Nanomaterials, including nanotubes and nanocomposite materials, upgrade the energy stockpiling limit and charge-release paces of these gadgets. The improvement of lightweight and high-limit energy capacity arrangements is fundamental for the headway of electric vehicles, convenient hardware, and network stockpiling.

The natural uses of nanomaterials highlight their true capacity in tending to worldwide difficulties. Nanotechnology offers imaginative answers for natural remediation, especially in water decontamination and air filtration. Nanoparticles can be intended to catch contaminations, and reactant nanoparticles can work with the debasement of pollutants, giving practical and proficient answers for tidying up dirtied conditions.

Biotechnology: Opening the Secrets of Existence with CRISPR

The progressive quality altering innovation referred to as CRISPR-Cas9 has arisen as a leap forward in biotechnology, offering phenomenal accuracy in changing the hereditary code of living life forms. This innovation, enlivened by the regular protection systems of microscopic organisms, can possibly change fields like medication, horticulture, and fundamental natural exploration.

In medication, CRISPR-Cas9 holds guarantee for treating hereditary issues by unequivocally altering the DNA arrangements liable for these circumstances. Scientists are investigating the utilization of CRISPR to address changes related with infections like cystic fibrosis, sickle cell iron deficiency, and strong dystrophy. The capacity to alter the human genome with accuracy opens new roads for creating designated treatments and possibly relieving hereditary infections.

The agrarian area is likewise ready to profit from CRISPR innovation. Specialists are investigating its application in creating crops with upgraded protection from vermin and illnesses, worked on dietary substance, and expanded yields. CRISPR considers the exact change of explicit qualities in plant genomes, offering an amazing asset for making crops that are stronger and can add to worldwide food security.

Notwithstanding its applications in medication and farming, CRISPR-Cas9 has turned into an imperative device in fundamental natural exploration. Researchers use

CRISPR to concentrate on the elements of explicit qualities, unwinding the secrets of cell processes and adding to how we might interpret life at the sub-atomic level. The simplicity and accuracy of CRISPR innovation have sped up the speed of logical revelation, empowering specialists to investigate and control the hereditary code with phenomenal productivity.

Man-made reasoning: The Ascent of AI and Brain Organizations

Man-made consciousness (artificial intelligence), especially AI and brain organizations, has encountered a flood in forward leaps that are reshaping enterprises and our day to day routines. AI calculations, propelled by the construction and capability of the human cerebrum, have shown momentous capacities in design acknowledgment, language handling, and direction.

One of the vital leap forwards in artificial intelligence is the improvement of profound learning calculations, a subset of AI that includes brain networks with numerous layers. Profound learning has made striking progress in errands, for example, picture acknowledgment, normal language handling, and game playing. This advancement has energized progressions in facial acknowledgment innovation, remote helpers, and independent vehicles.

Generative models, a class of AI calculations, have likewise taken critical steps. Generative ill-disposed networks (GANs), specifically, stand out for their capacity to create reasonable manufactured information. This advancement has applications in making exact pictures, improving information expansion procedures, and in any event, recreating practical situations for preparing simulated intelligence frameworks.

The crossing point of man-made intelligence with different fields, like medical care and money, has prompted leap forwards in prescient demonstrating and customized administrations. AI calculations can investigate huge measures of clinical information to distinguish designs and anticipate infection results, adding to additional exact analyses and treatment plans. In finance, computer based intelligence calculations dissect market patterns and make expectations, directing speculation choices and hazard the board systems.

Quantum Advances: Saddling the Force of Quantum Mechanics

Quantum innovations, outfitting the standards of quantum mechanics, have arisen as an outskirts with the possibility to change processing, correspondence, and detecting.

Quantum PCs, specifically, have the ability to perform complex estimations at speeds incomprehensible with traditional PCs.

Quantum figuring forward leaps incorporate the advancement of quantum processors with expanding quantities of qubits and further developed mistake amendment strategies. Organizations and examination establishments are hustling to accomplish "quantum matchless quality," where a quantum PC outflanks the most exceptional old style supercomputers in unambiguous undertakings. This achievement would check a change in outlook in computational capacities, opening additional opportunities in streamlining, cryptography, and materials disclosure.

2.3 The societal and economic impact of nanotechnology

The cultural and financial effect of nanotechnology is both significant and expansive, impacting different parts of our day to day routines, enterprises, and worldwide frameworks. As nanotechnology proceeds to advance and coordinate into different areas, its suggestions reach out from medical services to energy, materials science to gadgets, and then some. This account investigates the many-sided interchange among nanotechnology and society, analyzing the groundbreaking impacts on economies, ventures, and the manner in which we see and collaborate with the world.

Financial Scene: Nanotechnology as a Motor of Development

Nanotechnology has arisen as an impetus for financial development, encouraging advancement, making new businesses, and driving efficiency gains. State run administrations, perceiving its true capacity, have put vigorously in nanotechnology innovative work, prompting the foundation of committed research places and subsidizing drives. This essential speculation has impelled logical revelation as well as situated countries at the front line of the worldwide nanotechnology scene.

The monetary effect of nanotechnology is obvious in the development of new business sectors and ventures. Nanomaterials, with their one of a kind properties, have tracked down applications in a bunch of areas, from hardware to medical services, making financial worth and producing business valuable open doors. As the interest for nanotechnology-empowered items and administrations keeps on rising, it animates monetary action and adds to the development of arising businesses.

Besides, nanotechnology assumes a significant part in improving the seriousness of customary businesses. The joining of nanomaterials into existing assembling processes works on the exhibition and usefulness of items. For example, the utilization of nanocomposites in materials fabricating brings about more grounded, lighter, and more tough items, encouraging advancement and keeping up with the seriousness of businesses in the worldwide market.

The monetary effect of nanotechnology reaches out past modern applications to envelop the medical services area. Nanomedicine, with its true capacity for customized and designated treatments, has made another wilderness in medical services conveyance. The advancement of nanoscale drug conveyance frameworks, demonstrative devices, and imaging specialists has worked on quiet results as well as animated financial action in the drug and medical care businesses.

Notwithstanding immediate monetary commitments, nanotechnology cultivates development biological systems that produce a far reaching influence across different areas. Joint efforts between the scholarly community, industry, and government establishments make prolific ground for cutting edge disclosures and innovative headways. This cooperative methodology advances information move, innovative exercises, and the foundation of new companies, further enhancing the financial effect of nano-technology.

Medical care Transformation: Nanomedicine and Customized Therapies

Nanotechnology's effect on medical care is progressive, introducing another period of diagnostics, drug conveyance, and restorative mediations. The accuracy managed by controlling materials at the nanoscale has converted into leap forwards that can possibly change the analysis and treatment of illnesses.

In diagnostics, nanotechnology has empowered the improvement of profoundly delicate and explicit devices for distinguishing biomarkers related with different illnesses. Nanosensors, frequently founded on standards of surface plasmon reverberation or quantum dabs, take into account the early discovery of infections at the sub-atomic level. This groundbreaking ability holds guarantee for early finding, customized treatment designs, and worked on tolerant results.

Nanotechnology has likewise upset drug conveyance, a foundation of medical services. Nanoparticles and nanocarriers can be designed to move restorative specialists with accuracy to explicit cells or tissues, upgrading the adequacy of medicines. This designated drug conveyance approach limits secondary effects, lessens the expected dose, and works on persistent consistence, tending to longstanding difficulties in drug advancement.

Additionally, nanotechnology has opened new boondocks in disease treatment. Nanoparticles can be intended to target malignant growth cells, conveying restorative specialists straightforwardly to the site of the growth specifically. This designated approach limits harm to sound tissues, improves the adequacy of therapies like chemo-therapy, and adds to the advancement of more mediocre and customized malignant growth treatments.

The cultural effect of these headways is significant. Patients benefit from additional successful and less obtrusive medicines, prompting worked on personal satisfaction. The shift toward customized medication, worked with by nanotechnology, lines up with a patient-focused approach, fitting medicines to individual qualities and heredi-tary profiles.

This change in outlook in medical services can possibly decrease the weight of illnesses, further develop wellbeing results, and add to the general prosperity of social orders.

Natural Manageability: Nanotechnology for a Greener Future

Nanotechnology assumes an essential part in addressing worldwide difficulties connected with natural manageability. From contamination remediation to energy effectiveness, nanotechnology offers inventive arrangements that add to a greener and more manageable future.

In ecological remediation, nanomaterials display extraordinary adsorption and syn-ergist properties that make them successful devices for tidying up contaminated air, water, and soil. Nanoparticles, for example, graphene oxide and metal oxides, can catch poisons, weighty metals, and pollutants, prompting further developed water quality and air filtration. The high surface region and reactivity of nanomaterials empower focused on and proficient remediation methodologies.

The utilization of nanotechnology in water treatment is especially imperative. Nanomaterials can be designed to eliminate contaminations, microorganisms, and poisons from water sources. The advancement of nanocomposite films for water filtration, able to do specifically permitting specific particles to go through, can possibly address water shortage issues and further develop admittance to clean drinking water.

In the energy area, nanotechnology adds to the advancement of economical energy arrangements. Nanomaterials upgrade the proficiency of sun based cells by working on light retention and charge transport, prompting headways in sun oriented energy advancements. Nanotechnology likewise assumes a vital part in energy capacity, with nanomaterials improving the exhibition of batteries and supercapacitors. These progressions add to the improvement of cleaner and more proficient energy frameworks.

The cultural effect of nanotechnology in natural manageability reaches out to the improvement of eco-accommodating items and cycles. Nanomaterials are integrated into coatings, materials, and building materials, giving functionalities, for example, self-cleaning surfaces and improved strength. The joining of nanotechnology into ordinary items lines up with the standards of green and reasonable advances, advancing naturally cognizant utilization designs.

Challenges and Moral Contemplations: Exploring the Nanotechnology Scene
While the cultural and financial effect of nanotechnology is certainly sure, it is critical to recognize and address related difficulties and moral contemplations. Wellbeing concerns with respect to the expected poisonousness of certain nanomaterials, both for human openness and natural effect, require thorough examination and administrative oversight. The extraordinary properties that make nanomaterials powerful likewise bring up issues about their drawn out impacts, provoking a careful way to deal with their sending.

Moral contemplations reach out past security worries to include issues of value, access, and cultural ramifications. As nanotechnology turns out to be progressively coordinated into different areas, questions emerge about who benefits from these headways and whether there are unseen side-effects that excessively influence specific populaces. Tending to these moral contemplations is critical for guaranteeing the dependable and evenhanded improvement of nanotechnology.

Straightforwardness and public commitment are fundamental parts of mindful nanotechnology advancement. Teaching people in general about the advantages and expected dangers of nanotechnology cultivates informed direction and advances a feeling of shared liability. Open and comprehensive exchanges including researchers, policymakers, ethicists, and general society add to the improvement of arrangements and guidelines that offset advancement with security and moral contemplations.

Purchaser Items and Regular daily existence: Nanotechnology in real life

The combination of nanotechnology into customer items has become progressively predominant, affecting different features of regular day to day existence. Nanomaterials track down applications in materials, gadgets, beauty care products, and food bundling, adding to the advancement of novel and further developed materials.

In materials, nanotechnology has led to textures with improved properties like water repellency, stain obstruction, and antimicrobial movement. Nanocoatings applied to materials give functionalities that work on the sturdiness and execution of attire, making items with added incentive for customers. The consolidation of nanomaterials into athletic apparel, outside gear, and ordinary dress epitomizes the groundbreaking effect of nanotechnology on the material business.

The hardware area has seen critical headways driven by nanotechnology. Nanoscale materials, like carbon nanotubes and graphene, have become essential parts of electronic gadgets. The scaling down of semiconductors and the improvement of nanoelectronic gadgets have prompted more modest, quicker.

Chapter 3

The Grey Goo Hypothesis

The Dark Goo Speculation, a speculative idea established in the domain of nano-technology, investigates a tragic situation where self-repeating nanobots, once released, multiply wildly, consuming all matter on The planet and changing it into a uniform, self-recreating mass frequently alluded to as "dim goo." This speculation, while gener-ally hypothetical and more lined up with sci-fi than prompt logical worries, digs into the potential dangers related with cutting edge nanotechnology, encouraging cautious thought of moral, wellbeing, and administrative measures.

The center thought of the Dim Goo Speculation imagines what is happening where nanobots, intended for explicit purposes like assembling or clinical applications, unintentionally get away from regulation and start to duplicate independently. These nanobots, outfitted with the capacity to self-reproduce and consume encompass-ing matter for unrefined components, go through remarkable development, at last prompting the change of Earth into an undifferentiated mass of nanomachines.

The beginning of the Dark Goo Speculation can be followed back to conversa-tions about the possible dangers and difficulties of nanotechnology. As researchers and scientists started investigating the conceivable outcomes of controlling matter at the nanoscale, concerns emerged with respect to the potentially negative side-effects of self-duplicating nanomachines. The expression "dim goo" was promoted by Eric Drexler, a trailblazer in the area of nanotechnology, in his book "Motors of Creation," where he illustrated both the commitments and expected entanglements of sub-atomic nanotechnology.

It is pivotal to perceive that the Dim Goo Theory is generally speculative and ought to be viewed as a low-likelihood, high-influence situation. The improvement of self-repeating nanobots with the capacity to consume all matter requires a degree of refinement and designing accuracy that goes past current innovative capacities. In any case, the speculation fills in as a useful example, provoking researchers and policy-makers to painstakingly consider the moral, wellbeing, and administrative parts of propelling nanotechnology.

One of the critical difficulties in evaluating the Dark Goo Speculation is the innate trouble in foreseeing the way of behaving of nanoscale frameworks, particularly those with self-repeating abilities. At the nanoscale, the principles of traditional material science give way to quantum impacts, presenting a degree of intricacy that makes it trying to precisely display and foresee the way of behaving of nanomachines. This intricacy highlights the requirement for a careful comprehension of nanoscale cooperations and hearty wellbeing measures.

The capable improvement of nanotechnology requires a multidisciplinary approach that consolidates experiences from material science, science, science, morals, and strategy. Scientists should team up to lay out rules and conventions that moderate the dangers related with self-repeating nanobots. While the Dim Goo Theory stays speculative, the potential outcomes warrant proactive measures to guarantee the protected and moral advancement of nanotechnology.

Moral contemplations encompassing nanotechnology reach out past the Dim Goo Speculation to incorporate more extensive worries connected with protection, security, and unseen side-effects. As nanotechnology turns out to be progressively incorporated into different areas, questions emerge about the expected abuse of nanomaterials and the moral ramifications of controlling matter at such a principal level.

Protection concerns might emerge with regards to nanoscale sensors and observation applications. Nanosensors, with the capacity to recognize explicit particles or accumulate data at the sub-atomic level, could be utilized for different purposes, including observation. The arrangement of nanoscale reconnaissance gadgets brings up moral issues about assent, protection privileges, and the potential for misuse.

Security concerns likewise arise in the improvement of nanomaterials with double use applications. Nanotechnology can possibly make progressed materials with remarkable properties, some of which might have military applications. The capable turn of events and sending of nanomaterials require cautious thought of the potential security suggestions and the foundation of global standards and arrangements to forestall abuse.

Potentially negative side-effects, while not really prompting a Dim Goo situation, present moral difficulties in the joining of nanotechnology into daily existence. The utilization of nanomaterials in purchaser items, for instance, brings up issues about long haul ecological effect and potential wellbeing chances. The moral obligation to completely survey and convey likely dangers to the general population is principal in guaranteeing the protected reception of nanotechnology.

From a moral point of view, straightforwardness and inclusivity are fundamental in the advancement of nanotechnology. Open exchange between researchers, policymakers, ethicists, and people in general can assist with tending to worries, encourage trust, and guarantee that the advantages of nanotechnology are impartially circulated. Drawing in with different partners takes into account a more extensive comprehension of moral contemplations and helps shape capable strategies that guide the turn of events and organization of nanotechnology.

Administrative systems assume a significant part in tending to moral and wellbeing concerns related with nanotechnology. State run administrations and worldwide associations need to lay out clear rules and guidelines for the dependable turn of events, testing, and sending of nanomaterials and nanodevices.

Administrative oversight guarantees that exploration and development in nanotechnology line up with moral standards and focus on human and natural wellbeing.

As the area of nanotechnology progresses, continuous examination is fundamental for better comprehend the possible dangers and advantages related with nanomaterials and nanodevices. Hearty gamble evaluations, combined with straightforward correspondence of discoveries, add to informed independent direction and mindful advancement. The prudent guideline, which supporters making a preventive move despite vulnerability, turns out to be especially significant with regards to nanotechnology, where the intricacy of nanoscale cooperations presents vulnerabilities.

Public mindfulness and schooling assume a critical part in the moral improvement of nanotechnology. By cultivating a comprehension of nanotechnology and its suggestions, society can effectively take part in the dynamic cycle and consider partners responsible. Instruction drives ought to expect to overcome any issues between logical headways and public grasping, engaging people to pursue informed decisions and add to the moral talk encompassing nanotechnology.

3.1 The concept of self-replicating nanobots

The idea of self-reproducing nanobots, arranged at the convergence of sci-fi and logical hypothesis, has enamored the creative mind of the two analysts and people in general. Coming from the more extensive area of nanotechnology, the thought spins around the advancement of nanoscale robots that have the capacity to repeat independently. While this idea holds critical potential for different applications, going from medication to assembling, it additionally brings up significant issues with respect to somewhere safe and secure, morals, and the possible unseen side-effects of releasing self-imitating elements at the nanoscale.

At its center, the idea of self-imitating nanobots imagines little machines, frequently on the size of nanometers, furnished with the capacity to recreate themselves. This limit with respect to independent generation draws motivation from natural frameworks, where cells partition and imitate to support life. In the domain of nanotechnology, specialists examine outfitting this crucial standard to make another class of machines with the possibility to change different fields.

One of the essential inspirations driving investigating self-repeating nanobots lies in the possibility of versatile and proficient assembling. Customary assembling processes are in many cases asset concentrated and tedious. The possibility of nanobots independently repeating and gathering complex designs offers a dream of profoundly effective and fast creation strategies. This might actually reform businesses, prompting the making of complex materials and gadgets with exceptional accuracy.

In medication, the idea of self-repeating nanobots presents the chance of designated drug conveyance and remedial mediations at the cell or sub-atomic level. Envision an armada of nanobots intended to recognize and kill malignant growth cells with unrivaled accuracy, or fix harmed tissues at the nanoscale. The potential for such clinical applications could introduce another period of customized and exceptionally successful medical services.

Nonetheless, the charm of self-recreating nanobots likewise raises critical worries, maybe most outstandingly embodied by the speculative situation known as the "Dim Goo." This Judgment day situation imagines what is happening where self-duplicating nanobots, once delivered into the climate, wildly consume all matter, changing Earth into a dark, dormant mass. While the Dark Goo situation remains exceptionally speculative and established more in sci-fi than logical reality, it highlights the requirement for cautious thought of the potential dangers related with self-recreating nanobots.

One basic test in acknowledging self-duplicating nanobots lies in the mind boggling balance among independence and control. Making nanobots fit for independent replication requests a degree of refinement in designing and programming that surpasses current mechanical capacities. Besides, guaranteeing that these nanobots imitate unequivocally and just under determined conditions is a considerable errand. Finding some kind of harmony is fundamental to forestall unseen side-effects and expected chances.

Wellbeing concerns encompassing self-reproducing nanobots stretch out past the speculative Dim Goo situation. The potential for accidental natural effect and the cooperation of nanobots with living organic entities bring up moral and environmental issues. Could self-repeating nanobots unintentionally hurt environments or disturb the sensitive equilibrium of nature? Understanding and addressing these worries is vital to the capable turn of events and organization of nanotechnology.

Moral contemplations encompassing self-repeating nanobots include a scope of issues, from possible abuse and potentially negative results to inquiries regarding assent and straightforwardness. The sending of nanobots in different areas, including medication, producing, and natural remediation, requires hearty moral systems that focus on security, value, and responsibility.

Protection concerns likewise arise with regards to self-reproducing nanobots, especially in applications including observation or information assortment. The capacity of nanobots to explore complex conditions and accumulate data at the sub-atomic level brings up issues about the limits of protection and the moral ramifications of inescapable observation. Finding some kind of harmony between mechanical advancement and individual security privileges is a urgent part of dependable nanotechnology improvement.

Tending to the moral components of self-recreating nanobots requires straight-forwardness and inclusivity in dynamic cycles. Drawing in with a different scope of partners, including researchers, ethicists, policymakers, and people in general, guarantees that moral contemplations are totally assessed, and potential dangers are relieved. The capable advancement of self-duplicating nanobots requires a continuous exchange that thinks about the more extensive cultural ramifications of this arising innovation.

Administrative systems assume a significant part in molding the moral improvement of self-reproducing nanobots. State run administrations and worldwide associations should lay out clear rules and principles to oversee the exploration, testing, and organization of nanobots. Administrative oversight guarantees that moral standards are coordinated into the advancement interaction and that potential dangers are evaluated and tended to before broad reception.

Public mindfulness and training are urgent parts of the moral talk encompassing self-repeating nanobots. As these ideas move from the domain of logical hypothesis to likely certifiable applications, it is basic to instruct the general population about the advantages, gambles, and moral contemplations related with this innovation. Informed public talk enables people to add to dynamic cycles and considers partners responsible for dependable nanotechnology advancement.

The expected utilizations of self-repeating nanobots in medication present a change in perspective in medical services. The capacity to convey nanobots for designated drug conveyance, diagnostics, and remedial intercessions at the cell or sub-atomic level holds the commitment of upsetting clinical medicines. Envision a situation where nanobots, modified to perceive explicit markers related with sicknesses, explore the circulation system to convey helpful specialists unequivocally where required, limiting secondary effects and enhancing therapy results.

In drug conveyance, self-imitating nanobots could address a portion of the long-standing difficulties of conventional medication organization. Nanobots intended to help remedial payloads could explore through the many-sided pathways of the human body with exceptional accuracy. This designated drug conveyance approach could upgrade the viability of medicines while limiting the effect on sound tissues, a huge improvement over traditional fundamental medication conveyance techniques.

Symptomatic uses of self-reproducing nanobots offer the potential for right on time and exact recognition of infections. Nanobots outfitted with sensors fit for rec-ognizing explicit biomarkers related with different circumstances could give constant data about the condition of the body. This early analytic ability could change illness the board, empowering mediations at the earliest stages and working on quiet results.

Remedial mediations at the nanoscale open new wildernesses for clinical medicines. Self-duplicating nanobots could be modified to fix harmed tissues, recover organs, or even objective and kill disease cells with unmatched accuracy. The potential for customized and profoundly compelling clinical mediations proclaims another time in medical services, where therapies are custom-made to individual hereditary profiles and illness attributes.

Notwithstanding the groundbreaking capability of self-recreating nanobots in medication, huge difficulties and moral contemplations should be tended to. The intricacy of human science and the expected connections among nanobots and living creatures require careful exploration and hazard appraisals. Guaranteeing the well-being and adequacy of these nanobots in the human body is principal to their mindful coordination into clinical practice.

Natural uses of self-duplicating nanobots revolve around their likely job in remediation, contamination control, and ecological observing. The capacity of nanobots to explore complex conditions and connect at the sub-atomic level opens opportunities for focused on and proficient ecological mediations.

In contamination control, self-duplicating nanobots could be designed to target and kill explicit poisons. For instance, nanobots outfitted with reactant capacities could work with the breakdown of destructive substances, adding to the remediation of polluted air, water, or soil. The accuracy and designated nature of these mediations could altogether improve the effectiveness of ecological cleanup endeavors.

Ecological checking presents another expected application, where self-repeating nanobots could be conveyed to accumulate continuous information on contamination levels, environment wellbeing, and environment factors. Outfitted with sensors equipped for identifying explicit ecological markers, these nanobots could give significant experiences into the condition of the climate. The information gathered could illuminate proof based decision-production for supportable asset the executives and ecological protection.

Nonetheless, the organization of self-duplicating nanobots in the climate raises moral and security concerns. The potential for accidental environmental outcomes and the collaboration of nanobots with normal biological systems require a mindful and informed approach. Far reaching risk appraisals, ecological effect studies, and administrative structures are crucial for guide the responsible.

3.2 The "grey goo" scenario and its origins

The "dim goo" situation, an idea that has penetrated conversations inside the domain of nanotechnology, summons a tragic vision where self-recreating nanobots, once released, multiply wildly, consuming all matter on The planet and changing it into a uniform, self-duplicating mass frequently alluded to as "dim goo."

While this situation is to a great extent hypothetical and dwells more in the space of sci-fi than a quick logical concern, it fills in as a useful example and prompts a more profound investigation of the potential dangers related with cutting edge nanotechnology.

The starting points of the "dark goo" situation can be followed back to conversations about the difficulties and dangers of nanotechnology. In the mid 1980s, Eric Drexler, a spearheading figure in the area of nanotechnology, presented the idea in his book "Motors of Creation." Drexler imagined a future where nanoscale machines, or nanobots, furnished with the capacity to self-reproduce, could unintentionally get away from control and gone crazy, consuming all matter in their way.

The expression "dim goo" itself distinctively embodies the envisioned result of such a situation - a world decreased to a dormant, shapeless mass of nanomachines, looking like a dim gooey substance. This speculative circumstance turned into a point of convergence in conversations about the likely dangers and moral contemplations encompassing nanotechnology, stressing the requirement for cautious assessment and mindful turn of events.

The "dim goo" situation spins around the possibility of self-reproducing nanobots intended for explicit purposes, like assembling or clinical applications, getting away from their controlled surroundings and imitating independently. In this situation, the nanobots would use accessible assets, including natural matter, to fuel their replication cycle. The remarkable development of these nanobots would prompt the uncontrolled change of all matter into a uniform, self-reproducing mass - the dim goo.

While the "dim goo" situation has caught the creative mind of the general population and energized conversations about the possible dangers of nanotechnology, it is fundamental to underline that it remains to a great extent speculative. The improvement of self-recreating nanobots with the capacity to consume all matter requires a degree of refinement and designing accuracy that surpasses current innovative capacities. Besides, mainstream researchers is keenly conscious about the potential dangers related with nanotechnology and is effectively participated in examination to comprehend and moderate these dangers.

One of the essential difficulties in assessing the "dark goo" situation is the intricacy of nanoscale frameworks and their way of behaving. At the nanoscale, the guidelines of old style physical science give way to quantum impacts, presenting a degree of eccentricism that makes it trying to precisely display and foresee the way of behaving of nanomachines. The innate intricacy of nanoscale communications highlights the requirement for intensive examination and chance evaluations to direct the mindful advancement of nanotechnology.

The idea of self-recreating nanobots, which frames the premise of the "dark goo" situation, is established in the standards of sub-atomic nanotechnology.

Sub-atomic nanotechnology imagines the exact control of issue at the sub-atomic and nuclear levels to make new materials, gadgets, and frameworks with uncommon functionalities. The possibility of self-imitating nanobots draws motivation from organic frameworks, where cells recreate to support life.

In the domain of nanotechnology, scientists investigate the capability of making nanomachines that copy the replication components tracked down in living life forms. The objective is to saddle these replication abilities for different applications, going from medication to assembling. Self-recreating nanobots could, in principle, offer a clever way to deal with versatile assembling, proficient medication conveyance, and other extraordinary advancements.

In medication, the idea of self-imitating nanobots holds the commitment of reforming drug conveyance and remedial mediations. Envision nanobots customized to recognize and target disease cells with unrivaled accuracy, conveying remedial specialists straightforwardly to the site of the growth. The potential for designated drug conveyance at the nanoscale could limit aftereffects and improve the adequacy of medicines.

In assembling, self-recreating nanobots could introduce another period of effective and quick creation techniques. The capacity of nanobots to independently repeat and collect complex designs could alter conventional assembling processes. This vision of nanobots building mind boggling materials and gadgets at the nanoscale opens opportunities for progressions in materials science and the production of novel advances.

While the expected uses of self-recreating nanobots are convincing, the "dark goo" situation highlights the requirement for cautious thought of the related dangers. The speculative situation imagines what is going on where the advantages of self-recreating nanobots become eclipsed by the wild multiplication and change of issue, prompting devastating results.

Wellbeing concerns encompassing self-reproducing nanobots stretch out past the "dim goo" situation to include more extensive moral and natural contemplations. The potential for accidental natural effect and the collaboration of nanobots with living creatures bring up issues about the capable turn of events and arrangement of nanotechnology. Understanding and addressing these worries are fundamental to guaranteeing the protected coordination of nanotechnology into different areas.

From a moral stance, straightforwardness and inclusivity are pivotal in the improvement of self-imitating nanobots. Open discourse between researchers, policymakers, ethicists, and general society adds to informed direction and guarantees that moral contemplations are completely assessed. Drawing in with different partners considers a more complete comprehension of moral ramifications and helps shape mindful strategies that guide the turn of events and sending of self-repeating nanobots.

Administrative structures assume a significant part in tending to moral and wellbeing concerns related with self-imitating nanobots. States and worldwide associations need to lay out clear rules and principles for the mindful turn of events, testing, and sending of nanobots. Administrative oversight guarantees that exploration and development in nanotechnology line up with moral standards and focus on human and ecological wellbeing.

Public mindfulness and training are critical parts of the moral talk encompassing self-reproducing nanobots. As these ideas move from the domain of logical hypothesis to expected certifiable applications, it is basic to teach the general population about the advantages, gambles, and moral contemplations related with this innovation.

Informed public talk engages people to add to dynamic cycles and considers partners responsible for dependable nanotechnology improvement.

Tending to the "dim goo" situation and its related dangers requires a multidisciplinary approach that includes researchers, ethicists, policymakers, and general society. Continuous investigation into the wellbeing and ecological effect of nanomaterials, combined with administrative structures that guarantee moral and fair practices, is critical. The straightforward correspondence of logical progressions and their suggestions to the public cultivates a feeling of shared liability and informed independent direction.

3.3 Understanding the mechanisms behind the threat

Understanding the components behind the likely danger of self-recreating nanobots, especially with regards to the "dim goo" situation, requires a nuanced investigation of the hidden standards of nanotechnology and the difficulties related with designing at the nanoscale. While the idea of self-reproducing nanobots draws motivation from the perplexing cycles of organic replication, making an interpretation of these standards into practical nanomachines presents huge logical and designing difficulties.

At the core of the "dark goo" situation is the possibility that self-duplicating nanobots, once released, could go through uncontrolled expansion, consuming all suitable matter and changing it into a uniform, self-recreating mass. To comprehend the components behind this likely danger, it is urgent to dive into the standards of self-replication, the nanoscale connections that administer these cycles, and the shields important to forestall potentially negative results.

Self-replication at the nanoscale includes the independent proliferation of nanobots, drawing motivation from natural frameworks where cells partition and duplicate to support life. The imagined nanobots would have the capacity to duplicate by using encompassing materials as assets, energizing the replication cycle. While the idea is captivating and offers possible advantages for versatile assembling and clinical applications, it presents complex difficulties that should be addressed to relieve the dangers related with uncontrolled replication.

One of the essential difficulties lies in designing nanobots with the ability for independent replication. Current mechanical abilities miss the mark regarding making nanomachines that can exactly duplicate themselves with the degree of complexity imagined in the "dim goo" situation. Accomplishing such accuracy at the nanoscale requires a profound comprehension of sub-atomic collaborations, the improvement of cutting edge materials, and the capacity to control nanoscale processes with remarkable precision.

Moreover, guaranteeing that self-imitating nanobots reproduce just under indicated conditions is a considerable errand. The potential for unseen side-effects emerges if nanobots recreate wildly in uncontrolled conditions. Creating safeguard components and programming shields is fundamental to forestall the situation where nanobots get away from control and multiply wildly.

The intricacy of nanoscale associations adds one more layer of challenge to understanding the components behind the likely danger of self-duplicating nanobots. At the nanoscale, the way of behaving of materials digresses from old style physical science, and quantum impacts become possibly the most important factor. Foreseeing and controlling the way of behaving of nanomachines at this scale requires an intensive comprehension of quantum mechanics, sub-atomic elements, and the one of a kind properties of nanomaterials.

Quantum impacts, for example, burrowing and snare, present a degree of capriciousness that makes it trying to demonstrate and foresee the way of behaving of nanoscale frameworks precisely. The transaction of quantum impacts with the intricacy of nanoscale cooperations raises worries about the potential for surprising ways of behaving in self-imitating nanobots, stressing the requirement for exhaustive examination and hazard evaluations.

The capable improvement of nanotechnology, including self-recreating nanobots, requires a multidisciplinary approach that incorporates experiences from physical science, science, science, and materials science. Specialists working in nanotechnology should team up to acquire an all encompassing comprehension of nanoscale connections and foster hearty security estimates that record for the extraordinary difficulties presented by the quantum impacts at play.

Tending to the likely danger of self-imitating nanobots requires an extensive gamble appraisal that assesses the natural, wellbeing, and security ramifications of these nanomachines. Understanding the potential dangers implies analyzing the connections among nanobots and living creatures, the effect on environments, and the drawn out results of uncontrolled replication.

Ecological worries include the potential for accidental environmental outcomes if self-duplicating nanobots were to connect with normal biological systems. The independent replication and utilization of assets could upset the fragile equilibrium of biological systems, influencing biodiversity and possibly prompting flowing ecological impacts. Thorough natural effect appraisals are essential to distinguish and relieve these likely dangers.

The association of self-repeating nanobots with living creatures presents wellbeing and security concerns. The exact instruments by which nanobots could interface with natural frameworks, whether incidentally or purposefully, require exhaustive examination. Inquiries regarding the possible harmfulness of nanomaterials, the impacts on cell capabilities, and the drawn out wellbeing suggestions should be tended to through thorough trial and error and testing.

Security measures to forestall potentially negative results incorporate the advancement of regulation conventions and safeguard systems. Designing nanobots with self-deactivation components or programming them to imitate just in controlled conditions are possible systems to alleviate the dangers of uncontrolled multiplication.

Examination into these security measures is essential to the capable advancement of self-imitating nanobots.

Moral contemplations encompassing the expected danger of self-recreating nanobots stretch out past the logical and specialized viewpoints to envelop more extensive cultural ramifications. The sending of nanobots in different areas, including medication, fabricating, and natural applications, brings up issues about value, access, and the potential for unseen side-effects that lopsidedly influence specific populaces.

Guaranteeing the moral advancement of self-reproducing nanobots requires straightforwardness and inclusivity in dynamic cycles. Drawing in with a different scope of partners, including researchers, ethicists, policymakers, and the general population, guarantees that moral contemplations are entirely assessed, and potential dangers are moderated. Capable advancement in nanotechnology requires a continuous exchange that thinks about the more extensive cultural ramifications of this arising innovation.

Administrative systems assume a critical part in tending to moral and security concerns related with self-recreating nanobots. State run administrations and worldwide associations should lay out clear rules and guidelines to administer the exploration, testing, and sending of nanobots. Administrative oversight guarantees that moral standards are coordinated into the improvement cycle and that potential dangers are evaluated and tended to before far and wide reception.

Public mindfulness and training are vital parts of the moral talk encompassing the likely danger of self-imitating nanobots. As these ideas move from the domain of logical hypothesis to possible genuine applications, it is basic to instruct people in general about the advantages, chances, and moral contemplations related with this innovation. Informed public talk engages people to add to dynamic cycles and considers partners responsible for capable nanotechnology improvement.

The investigation of self-repeating nanobots likewise prompts a reflection on the more extensive ramifications of propelling innovation and the moral obligation of established researchers. As scientists push the limits of what is innovatively plausible, they should wrestle with the moral components of their work and consider the likely results of releasing independent, self-imitating substances into the world.

All in all, understanding the systems behind the possible danger of self-recreating nanobots, especially with regards to the "dim goo" situation, requires a thorough investigation of the logical, specialized, and moral elements of nanotechnology. The difficulties of designing nanobots equipped for independent replication, the intricacies of nanoscale communications, and the possible dangers to the climate and human wellbeing require a cautious and multidisciplinary approach.

The capable improvement of self-duplicating nanobots requests progressing research, risk evaluations, and the foundation of powerful security measures. Moral contemplations, including straightforwardness, inclusivity, and administrative systems, are indispensable to directing the turn of events and arrangement of nanotechnology.

As society explores the outskirts of nanotechnology, it is crucial for offset development with moral obligation, guaranteeing that the groundbreaking capability of self-recreating nanobots is acknowledged in a way that focuses on security, value, and the prosperity of both mankind and the climate.

Chapter 4

From Fiction to Reality

In the tremendous region of human creative mind, the line among fiction and reality has forever been a sensitive, consistently moving limit. The domain of probability, once bound to the pages of books and the cinema, has ventured into a complicated embroidery where the strings of creative mind and development weave flawlessly together. As we explore the 21st hundred years, the extension among fiction and reality has become more substantial than any other time in recent memory, introducing a period where the fantastical is not generally bound to the domains of fantasy and pretend.

The excursion from fiction to the truth is a demonstration of the dauntless human soul and the determined quest for the unexplored world. A story traverses hundreds of years, set apart by snapshots of creativity, logical leap forwards, and the intermingling of dissimilar fields of information. In this steadily developing story, the limits of what was once considered unthinkable keep on obscuring, making a scene where the once-unfathomable turns into the establishment for the following flood of progress.

One of the most convincing instances of this shift from fiction to the truth is the appearance of man-made brainpower (computer based intelligence). Once consigned to the domain of sci-fi, simulated intelligence has arisen as a strong power molding the direction of human turn of events. The thought of machines having human-like insight, fit for learning and adjusting, was once the stuff of Isaac Asimov's accounts. Today, a reality saturates each feature of our lives, from voice-enacted remote helpers to refined calculations molding our internet based encounters.

The development of simulated intelligence isn't simply a mechanical achievement; it is a demonstration of mankind's capacity to transform the theoretical into the substantial. What was once a speculative idea in the pages of books and the casings of movies is presently a universal presence, impacting how we work, convey, and explore the world. The excursion from imagining clever machines in fiction to making them in actuality has reshaped enterprises as well as provoked significant inquiries regarding the moral ramifications of this recently discovered power.

As we navigate this scene of obscured limits, the crossing point of science and innovation stands apart as one more exceptional part in the account of fiction turned reality. Upgrading the human body with mechanical increases, long a staple of sci-fi, has progressed into a blossoming field of logical investigation. The merging of man and machine, when the space of cyberpunk books, is currently an unmistakable possibility with improvements in prosthetics, brain interfaces, and hereditary designing.

The idea of bionic appendages, fit for reestablishing capability as well as giving improved capacities, reflects the computerized upgrades portrayed in fiction. However, the truth outperforms the creative mind, with prosthetics that answer brain signals, offering a degree of finesse and regular development recently thought out of reach. Also, brain interfaces that overcome any issues between the human cerebrum and outer gadgets open new roads for correspondence and control, suggestive of the brain jacks depicted in speculative fiction.

The intermingling of science and innovation stretches out past actual improvements, digging into the domain of hereditary designing. The planning of the human genome, when an aggressive logical undertaking, is presently a reality that has opened the possibility to alter and control the very constructing blocks of life. The idea of creator babies, a staple of tragic fiction, is currently a subject of moral discussion as headways in quality altering advances raise the chance of choosing and changing characteristics in unborn youngsters.

In the domain of room investigation, the excursion from fiction to reality has been set apart by great accomplishments and a reestablished feeling of enormous interest. The fantasy of interplanetary travel, once bound to the pages of sci-fi books, is currently a substantial objective for both legislative space organizations and confidential ventures. The colonization of Mars, an idea that filled the minds of scholars and movie producers, is presently a serious undertaking with plans and missions in different transformative phases.

Progressions in drive frameworks, mechanical technology, and manageable life support advancements have changed the fantasy about turning into a multi-planetary animal varieties into a sensible possibility. Privately owned businesses, driven by visionaries like Elon Musk, are effectively pursuing making mankind a multi-planetary animal categories. The story of room investigation, when overwhelmed by fictitious stories of interstellar experiences, is currently being written in the research centers and platforms of the present.

The account of fiction transforming into the truth isn't restricted to the domains of innovation and space investigation. The socio-political scene has likewise seen a change that repeats the tragic and idealistic dreams depicted in writing. The idea of a globalized world, interconnected through innovation and correspondence, was once the space of speculative fiction. Today, a reality has reshaped economies, societies, and the actual texture of human collaboration.

The ascent of the web, when a fantastical idea portrayed in cyberpunk books, has introduced a period of remarkable network. The advanced domain is presently an essential piece of daily existence, obscuring the lines between the physical and virtual universes. Virtual entertainment, when an idea consigned to the pages of sci-fi, is currently a strong power molding public talk, political developments, and individual characters.

The account of fiction transforming into the truth isn't generally one of consistent advancement and unrestrained positive thinking. It is additionally set apart by wake up calls and moral problems that drive us to go up against the results of our developments. The tragic dreams of observation states, obtrusive advances, and loss of protection portrayed in fiction are presently reverberated in the real factors of mass reconnaissance, information breaks, and the moral ramifications of arising innovations.

The approach of biometric recognizable proof, facial acknowledgment, and prescient calculations has raised worries about the disintegration of individual security and the potential for maltreatment by strong elements. The moral contemplations encompassing the utilization of simulated intelligence in dynamic cycles, from law enforcement to monetary frameworks, mirror the need to explore the barely recognizable difference among advancement and responsibility. The story of fiction transforming into reality fills in as a preventative update that the ability to shape what's in store accompanies the obligation to think about its suggestions.

In the domain of natural supportability, the story of fiction transforming into reality takes on a need to get going. The portrayals of tragic scenes, biological breakdown, and the outcomes of unrestrained industrialization in fiction are reflected in the natural difficulties confronting the planet today. The idea of environmentally friendly power sources, when a speculative thought, is currently a urgent part of worldwide endeavors to moderate environmental change and progress towards a manageable future.

The excursion from fiction to the truth is certainly not a direct movement yet a dynamic and multi-layered investigation of human potential. It is a story formed by the intermingling of creative mind, logical revelation, and cultural development. The difficulties and potential open doors introduced by this continuous story require a nuanced comprehension of the intricate transaction between mechanical development, moral contemplations, and the aggregate desires of humankind.

As we explore the steadily moving scene of fiction transforming into the real world, the job of training and social accounts becomes foremost. The narratives we tell, whether in writing, film, or different types of creative articulation, shape our view of the world and impact the direction of logical and mechanical advancement. The force of narrating to motivate advancement, encourage moral mindfulness, and imagine elective fates highlights the interconnectedness of fiction and reality.

All in all, the excursion from fiction to the truth is a demonstration of the unlimited capability of human creative mind and the ability to transform dreams into unmistakable accomplishments. From the domains of computer based intelligence and biotechnology to space investigation and cultural changes, the story of fiction transforming into the truth is a dynamic and continuous investigation of being human.

As we explore the intricacies of the 21st 100 years, the interchange among fiction and reality keeps on molding the account of our aggregate process into the unexplored world.

4.1 The evolution of the "grey goo" concept from science fiction

The idea of "dim goo" in sci-fi addresses a terrible vision of a future where self-reproducing nanobots consume all matter on The planet, decreasing it to a dead, homogeneous mass. This prophetically catastrophic situation, frequently portrayed in speculative fiction, has its foundations in both logical creative mind and worries about the potential dangers related with cutting edge nanotechnology. As we investigate the advancement of the "dark goo" idea, we dive into its beginnings in writing, its associations with genuine logical conversations on nanotechnology, and the continuous moral contemplations encompassing the improvement of self-reproducing nanomachines.

The expression "dark goo" itself was promoted by the English nanotechnologist Eric Drexler in his book "Motors of Creation: The Approaching Time of Nanotechnology," distributed in 1986. In this pivotal work, Drexler imagined a future where nanoscale machines, fit for self-replication, could winding wild, consuming every accessible asset and changing the Earth into a uniform mass of dim goo. Drexler's depiction of this horrendous situation filled in as a wake up call, encouraging researchers, policymakers, and the general population to think about the likely dangers and moral ramifications of propelling nanotechnology.

Drexler's conceptualization of the "dark goo" drew motivation from prior works of sci-fi, where comparative topics of out of control self-replication and wild nanobots were investigated. Eminently, the possibility of self-imitating machines traces all the way back to the mid-twentieth 100 years, with mathematician and PC researcher John von Neumann proposing the idea of a widespread constructor — a machine fit for replicating itself — during the 1940s. While von Neumann's thoughts were more centered around unique numerical ideas and software engineering, they laid the basis for later conversations about self-repeating machines, remembering those for the domain of nanotechnology.

The combination of logical hypothesis and sci-fi established the groundwork for the "dark goo" idea to catch the public creative mind. The possibility of little machines, undetectable to the unaided eye, quickly duplicating and consuming everything in their way, hit home for both the interest and apprehension about the unexplored world. As the idea got some forward movement, it tracked down its direction into a horde of sci-fi stories, solidifying its status as a preventative saying in conversations about the expected risks of cutting edge innovation.

In the domain of writing, the "dark goo" idea has been highlighted in different works, adding to its getting through presence in mainstream society. Michael Crichton's book

"Prey," distributed in 2002, investigates a situation where a haze of nanobots, initially intended for modern purposes, develops into a danger that jeopardizes all life.

Crichton's story handily winds around together components of tension and logical hypothesis, taking advantage of the nerves encompassing the potentially negative side-effects of logical trial and error.

The idea likewise tracked down its direction into Neal Stephenson's "The Precious stone Age," distributed in 1995, where self-recreating nanobots assume a huge part in forming the clever's modern world. Stephenson's work digs into the cultural ramifications of nanotechnology, investigating what it could mean for power elements, schooling, and the actual texture of human development. The consideration of the "dim goo" theme in Stephenson's account mirrors the continuous interest with the likely risks of uncontrolled nanomachines.

While the "dim goo" idea has penetrated the domain of fiction, its advancement has not been restricted to speculative narrating. Mainstream researchers, roused to some degree by the creative situations introduced in fiction, has taken part in serious conversations about the plausibility and dangers related with self-duplicating nano-machines.

In reality, nanotechnology includes controlling materials and gadgets at the nano-scale, regularly in the scope of 1 to 100 nanometers. The field has shown huge commitment in different applications, from medication and gadgets to materials science and energy. In any case, likewise with any strong innovation, worries about unseen side-effects and moral contemplations go with the possible advantages.

The possibility of self-duplicating nanobots brings up key issues about control, wellbeing, and the potential for accidental natural effects. While the "dim goo" situation introduced in fiction is a limit and impossible result, the chance of potentially negative side-effects stays a genuine worry in established researchers. Analysts and ethicists the same wrestle with the difficulties of creating rules and protects to alleviate the dangers related with the multiplication of self-duplicating nanomachines.

One of the essential difficulties in the improvement of self-repeating nanobots is guaranteeing that they can be controlled and customized to act in an anticipated and gainful way. The actual embodiment of self-replication infers a limit with regards to independence and transformation, qualities that, while possibly not painstakingly made due, could prompt unseen side-effects. Specialists dealing with nanotechnology should find some kind of harmony between bridling the capability of self-replication for useful purposes and carrying out shields to forestall bothersome results.

Moral contemplations likewise pose a potential threat in conversations about the turn of events and sending of nanotechnology. The possibility of making nano-machines that can work independently brings up issues about liability, responsibility, and the potential for abuse. As researchers dig further into the domain of nanotech-nology, the requirement for moral systems that guide innovative work turns out to be progressively basic.

The "dark goo" idea, while a sensationalized and outrageous vision, fills in as an important standard for moral conversations encompassing nanotechnology. It prompts researchers and policymakers to consider the more extensive ramifications of their work, empowering a proactive way to deal with tending to likely dangers before they emerge. As the area of nanotechnology keeps on progressing, continuous exchange and joint effort between researchers, ethicists, and policymakers are fundamental to guaranteeing that the advantages of this innovation are acknowledged without forfeiting wellbeing and moral guidelines.

Past the logical and moral contemplations, the "dim goo" idea has likewise saturated the domain of public talk and mainstream society, forming view of nanotechnology and affecting public perspectives. The depiction of horrendous situations in fiction, combined with media inclusion of logical progressions, adds to a more extensive story that outlines nanotechnology as a two sided deal — a device with massive potential yet in addition full of risk.

Public mindfulness and comprehension of nanotechnology assume a vital part in molding cultural perspectives and impacting the bearing of innovative work. The "dim goo" idea, as a wake up call, fills in as an emblematic portrayal of the potential entanglements related with unrestrained mechanical progression. It highlights the significance of capable development and the requirement for straightforwardness in imparting the dangers and advantages of arising advancements to people in general.

Amidst these conversations, it is fundamental to perceive the positive commitments that nanotechnology has made and keeps on making in different fields. From clinical applications, for example, designated drug conveyance and diagnostics to progressions in materials science that empower the making of additional productive and practical materials, nanotechnology can possibly reform different enterprises.

In medication, for instance, nanoscale materials and gadgets hold the commitment of additional exact and viable medicines. Designated drug conveyance frameworks, using nanocarriers, can convey prescriptions straightforwardly to explicit cells or tissues, limiting secondary effects and expanding helpful adequacy. Demonstrative strategies that influence nanoscale materials empower prior discovery of illnesses, working with opportune intercession and working on understanding results.

In materials science, the control of materials at the nanoscale has prompted the advancement of novel materials with upgraded properties. Nanocomposites, materials made out of nanoscale particles scattered in a lattice, display further developed strength, sturdiness, and conductivity contrasted with their mass partners. These progressions have suggestions for a great many businesses, from gadgets and aviation to energy and ecological supportability.

The development of the "dark goo" idea from sci-fi to logical talk highlights the complicated connection among creative mind and advancement. The wake up calls woven into the texture of speculative fiction act as guides, enlightening the potential entanglements that might lie ahead. As we explore the perplexing territory of arising advances, the examples got from these wake up calls guide us in producing a way that offsets progress with liability.

All in all, the advancement of the "dim goo" idea mirrors the powerful transaction between sci-fi, logical request, and moral contemplations in the domain of nanotechnology. From its beginnings in the creative domains of speculative fiction to its mix into certifiable conversations about the dangers and advantages of self-imitating nanomachines, the "dim goo" idea fills in as a multi-layered focal point through which we look at the convergence of human resourcefulness and the likely hazards of uncontrolled mechanical progression.

As we keep on propelling comprehension we might interpret nanotechnology and its applications, the examples drawn from the "dim goo" story stay important. They help us to remember the significance of capable advancement, moral contemplations, and proactive measures to guarantee.

4.2 Real-world concerns and discussions in the scientific community

In the consistently developing scene of logical investigation, genuine worries and conversations structure the bedrock whereupon headways are constructed. These worries envelop a range of issues, going from moral contemplations to down to earth difficulties, and they assume a vital part in forming the direction of logical examination and development. As we dig into the complexities of these true worries, we wind up at the crossing point of disclosure, obligation, and the complicated exchange among science and society.

One of the vital worries penetrating established researchers connects with the moral ramifications of arising advances. As forward leaps in fields like man-made brainpower, hereditary designing, and nanotechnology become progressively ordinary, the moral contemplations encompassing their applications become the overwhelming focus. Researchers, policymakers, and ethicists wrestle with questions that reach out past the lab, contemplating the cultural effects and moral components of their work.

In the domain of man-made reasoning (man-made intelligence), moral contemplations length a wide range, from worries about work dislodging because of robotization to issues of predisposition in algorithmic direction. As artificial intelligence frameworks become vital pieces of day to day existence, from independent vehicles to prescient examination in medical services, the requirement for moral rules becomes central. Conversations spin around straightforwardness, responsibility, and the fair and impartial organization of computer based intelligence advances to guarantee that their advantages are open to all citizenry.

Additionally, hereditary designing brings up significant moral issues, especially with regards to human genome altering. The capacity to control qualities makes the way for phenomenal conceivable outcomes, from annihilating genetic illnesses to upgrading mental capacities. Nonetheless, it additionally raises worries about the potential for fashioner children, where hereditary adjustments could be made to choose explicit characteristics. Mainstream researchers participates in continuous discoursed to lay out moral structures that balance the groundbreaking capability of hereditary design-ing with the need to forestall unseen side-effects and maintain moral standards.

Nanotechnology, with its commitment of controlling matter at the nanoscale, acquaints moral contemplations related with ecological effect and potentially negative results. The improvement of self-repeating nanobots, an idea that once dwelled immovably in the domain of sci-fi as the "dark goo" situation, prompts serious con-versations about the expected dangers of uncontrolled nanomachines. Ethicists and researchers team up to lay out rules that guarantee the capable turn of events and organization of nanotechnology, moderating the potential for ecological mischief and accidental aftereffects.

Past the moral aspects, functional difficulties likewise pose a potential threat in logical undertakings. Financing imperatives, asset restrictions, and the complexities of interdisciplinary coordinated effort address jumps that specialists should explore. The distribution of assets for logical exploration frequently contends with other cultural needs, and researchers should make convincing cases for the cultural worth of their work to get financing.

Interdisciplinary coordinated effort, while fundamental for handling complex diffi-culties, presents its own arrangement of difficulties. Different logical disciplines offer interesting viewpoints and techniques of real value, however consolidating these points of view into a strong system can be a fragile interaction. Powerful correspondence and coordinated effort across disciplines become basic for resolving multi-layered issues, from environmental change to general wellbeing emergencies.

The reproducibility emergency, an unavoidable worry in different logical fields, highlights the significance of thoroughness and straightforwardness in research. Inquiries regarding the dependability of logical discoveries have prompted expanded investigation of examination strategies and distribution rehearses. Specialists, diaries, and organizations wrestle with the need to lay out hearty guidelines for exploratory plan, information examination, and answering to guarantee the believability and replicability of logical investigations.

In the field of environment science, true worries take on a worldwide scale as researchers defy the dire difficulties of environmental change. The effects of increasing temperatures, outrageous climate occasions, and ocean level ascent require cooperative endeavors to comprehend, moderate, and adjust to the evolving environment.

Established researchers participates in conversations with policymakers and the general population to convey the seriousness of the circumstance and promoter for proof based arrangements that address the main drivers of environmental change.

Public commitment and correspondence arise as essential parts of tending to genuine worries in science. Researchers face the test of passing complex ideas on to general society, cultivating logical proficiency, and fighting falsehood. Overcoming any barrier between mainstream researchers and the more extensive public is fundamental for building trust, collecting support for research drives, and working with informed dynamic on issues that have sweeping ramifications for society.

In the domain of general wellbeing, the continuous worldwide reaction to irresistible illnesses highlights the interconnectedness of logical examination, public strategy, and cultural prosperity. The rise of novel microbes, for example, the SARS-CoV-2 infection answerable for the Coronavirus pandemic, requires fast and facilitated reactions from mainstream researchers. Antibody improvement, general wellbeing mediations, and the scattering of precise data become fundamental in defending general wellbeing.

Certifiable worries in established researchers stretch out to the area of room investigation. As mankind adventures past Earth, moral inquiries emerge in regards to the potential for planetary tainting. The quest for extraterrestrial life prompts cautious thought of conventions to try not to coincidentally acquaint Earth organic entities with other divine bodies or debasing logical instruments intended to distinguish indications of something going on under the surface somewhere else in the planetary group.

The moral ramifications of room investigation additionally reach out to the potential for space rock mining and asset extraction on divine bodies. As mechanical progressions make these undertakings more possible, conversations about mindful and supportable practices in space investigation gain conspicuousness. Adjusting the advantages of asset use with natural contemplations turns into a point of convergence in molding the eventual fate of room investigation.

This present reality concerns and conversations inside mainstream researchers are not detached from more extensive cultural issues, including those connected with variety, value, and incorporation. Established researchers wrestles with the requirement for expanded portrayal and equivalent open doors for people from underrepresented gatherings. Tending to fundamental hindrances and predispositions is fundamental for encouraging an academic local area that mirrors the variety of human encounters and points of view.

The elements of globalization likewise present genuine contemplations in logical examination. Joint efforts across borders work with the sharing of information and assets, however they likewise bring up issues about protected innovation, information sharing, and the impartial dispersion of logical advantages. The moral elements of worldwide logical organizations become especially remarkable while resolving issues with worldwide ramifications, for example, irresistible illnesses, environmental change, and admittance to fundamental innovations.

Certifiable worries in science are not static; they develop in light of progressions in innovation, changes in cultural needs, and arising difficulties. As logical information extends, so too does the obligation of established researchers to address the moral, commonsense, and cultural ramifications of its work. The iterative idea of logical request requires a consistent reassessment of approaches, procedures, and moral systems to line up with the developing scene of revelation.

All in all, this present reality concerns and conversations inside mainstream researchers structure a powerful embroidery that winds around together moral contemplations, useful difficulties, and cultural ramifications. From the moral components of man-made brainpower, hereditary designing, and nanotechnology to the down to earth difficulties of interdisciplinary coordinated effort, asset designation, and reproducibility, researchers explore a complicated landscape that requires a fragile equilibrium of development, obligation, and commitment with more extensive cultural worries.

As science keeps on propelling, this present reality worries at its very front highlight the requirement for a cooperative and comprehensive methodology. Moral contemplations should be woven into the texture of logical examination, directing the turn of events and utilization of new innovations. Viable difficulties request savvy fixes and a promise to straightforwardness and thoroughness. Drawing in with the general population, policymakers, and different viewpoints guarantees that the advantages of logical advancement are available and impartial.

Eventually, this present reality concerns and conversations inside mainstream researchers rise above the limits of labs and scholarly establishments. They shape the accounts of progress, obligation, and the common excursion of humankind as it explores the boondocks of information and addresses the squeezing difficulties of the present and future.

4.3 Science fiction's role in shaping public perception

Sci-fi, as a sort, stands firm on a novel footing in the scholarly and social scene. Past its diversion esteem, sci-fi assumes a crucial part in molding public discernment, impacting cultural perspectives toward science, innovation, and what's to come. This compelling power originates from the class' capacity to investigate inventive situations, extrapolate likely headways, and proposition a focal point through which crowds can mull over the effect of logical and innovative advancement on the human experience.

At its center, sci-fi capabilities as a psychological study, pushing the limits of what is known and investigating the domains of the unexplored world. Through stories set in far off prospects, substitute real factors, or speculative dreams of the present, sci-fi gives a stage to creators to imagine the results of logical disclosures and mechanical developments. This speculative nature permits the class to act as a proving ground for thoughts, both idealistic and tragic, offering a space for consideration and talk on the direction of human advancement.

The depiction of cutting edge innovations in sci-fi frequently goes before their acknowledgment in reality. Journalists and makers, powered by their creative mind and a comprehension of logical standards, present ideas that later turned into the establishment for innovative turns of events. For instance, the idea of a tablet PC, presently a pervasive gadget in current life, was predicted in sci-fi works some time before its genuine creation. The visionary idea of sci-fi subsequently empowers it to shape public assumptions and get ready society for the potential outcomes introduced by arising advancements.

The class' effect on open discernment reaches out past the domain of innovation to envelop more extensive cultural issues. Sci-fi stories frequently investigate the social, moral, and moral ramifications of logical headways, inciting crowds to think about the possible results of unrestrained advancement. Tragic dreams of extremist systems, environmental breakdown, or the abuse of innovation act as wake up calls, encouraging society to think about the moral components of logical development.

One of the getting through subjects in sci-fi is the investigation of computerized reasoning (artificial intelligence) and its effect on society. From Isaac Asimov's laws of mechanical technology to the pernicious HAL 9000 in Arthur C. Clarke's "2001: A Space Odyssey," sci-fi plays had a vital impact in forming public impression of man-made intelligence. The class has both energized interest with the possible capacities of smart machines and imparted a feeling of misgiving about the moral issues they might present. As genuine computer based intelligence progressions proceed, the impact of sci-fi on open perspectives toward artificial intelligence stays unmistakable, adding to continuous discussions about its joining into different parts of day to day existence.

Essentially, sci-fi has been a fruitful ground for investigating topics of room investigation and colonization. Works like H.G. Wells' "The Conflict of the Universes" and Arthur C. Clarke's "Meeting with Rama" have enraptured crowds with dreams of extraterrestrial life and the secrets of the universe. These accounts not just invigorate interest in the conceivable outcomes of room investigation yet in addition add to public talk on the moral and philosophical ramifications of human extension past Earth.

While sci-fi frequently investigates the likely advantages and traps of logical advancement, it likewise fills in as a mirror reflecting contemporary social issues. The class has been a vehicle for tending to subjects of personality, disparity, and equity.

Exemplary works like Philip K. Dick's "Do Androids Long for Electric Sheep?" (the reason for the film "Edge Sprinter") dive into inquiries of being human and the moral treatment of aware creatures, resembling contemporary conversations on sympathy, freedoms, and the treatment of minimized gatherings.

The visual medium, through sci-fi movies and TV series, further enhances the class' effect on open insight. Famous establishments like "Star Journey" have formed mainstream society as well as impacted cultural mentalities toward variety, incorporation, and collaboration. "Star Journey," with its hopeful vision of a future where mankind has beaten its divisions and works cooperatively with different outsider species, has filled in as an optimistic model for cultural concordance and solidarity.

Nonetheless, the impact of sci-fi can sometimes be negative or hopeful. Tragic accounts, for example, George Orwell's "1984" or Aldous Huxley's "State-of-the-art existence," act as wake up calls, advance notice against the risks of tyranny, observation, and loss of individual opportunities. These stories, while fictitious, resound with genuine nerves, affecting public talk on the harmony among security and protection, the job of innovation in administration, and the disintegration of individual freedoms.

The powerful connection between sci-fi and public insight is a two-way road. Similarly as sci-fi shapes public perspectives, it is likewise impacted by cultural qualities, fears, and goals. Creators and makers draw motivation from the general outlook, taking advantage of aggregate expectations and nerves to create accounts that resound with crowds. This cooperative relationship positions sci-fi as a social mirror that reflects, refracts, and shapes the developing cognizance of society.

In the domain of natural cognizance, sci-fi has progressively turned its look toward environmental subjects. Works like Kim Stanley Robinson's "Mars Set of three" and Paolo Bacigalupi's "The Water Blade" investigate the outcomes of ecological corruption, environmental change, and the battle for decreasing regular assets. These accounts add to the more extensive talk on manageability, asking crowds to consider the effect of human exercises in the world and imagine elective fates molded by naturally cognizant decisions.

The depiction of orientation and variety in sci-fi has likewise developed over the long run, reflecting and affecting cultural perspectives. Early sci-fi frequently showed orientation generalizations and needed different portrayal. In any case, contemporary works challenge these standards, highlighting complex characters who resist customary orientation jobs and address a range of personalities. This advancement lines up with more extensive social developments supporting for inclusivity and portrayal in media and then some.

As sci-fi draws in with issues of morals, innovation, and cultural elements, it fills in as a vehicle for moral reflection. The class prompts crowds to think about the outcomes of logical progressions and mechanical developments, cultivating an elevated familiarity with the moral aspects innate chasing information. Sci-fi urges a proactive way to deal with moral contemplations, encouraging society to lay out rules, guidelines, and moral structures that guide the mindful turn of events and utilization of arising innovations.

In the time of quick mechanical headway, the impact of sci-fi on open discernment stretches out to the domain of arising advancements like biotechnology and quality altering. Works like Kazuo Ishiguro's "Never Let Me Go" and the film "Gattaca" investigate the moral quandaries encompassing hereditary control, cloning, and the commodification of human existence. These accounts add to public conversations about the moral limits of controlling the human genome and the expected cultural results of such mediations.

The impact of sci-fi on open discernment is especially apparent in the talk encompassing mechanical technology and computerization. As mechanical technology innovation propels, inquiries regarding the effect on work, the economy, and human prosperity come to the bleeding edge. Sci-fi accounts, from Isaac Asimov's investigation of advanced mechanics morals to the humanoid robots in films like "I, Robot" and "Ex Machina," add to public getting it and worry about the joining of robots into different parts of society.

In exploring the convergence of sci-fi and public discernment, it is pivotal to perceive the class' ability to motivate and illuminate. Sci-fi fills in as a social gauge, reflecting cultural expectations, fears, and desires. It flashes discussions about the moral ramifications of logical progressions, prompts consideration about the future direction of humankind, and energizes a proactive position in forming the effect of innovation on society.

While sci-fi offers a focal point through which to investigate the outcomes of logical advancement, moving toward its stories with an insightful eye is fundamental. The class, while innovative, isn't a precious stone ball. It presents speculative situations that could conceivably line up with the real factors of arising advancements. As crowds draw in with sci-fi, it is pivotal to adjust the energy of visionary narrating with decisive reasoning, perceiving that what's in store is formed by mechanical advancement as well as by cultural decisions, moral contemplations, and aggregate activities.

All in all, sci-fi's part in molding public discernment is complex and significant. The class fills in as a course for investigating the ramifications of logical progressions, impacting cultural mentalities toward innovation, morals, and what's to come. From imagining the conceivable outcomes of room investigation to testing the moral problems of computerized reasoning and hereditary designing, sci-fi gives a material to examining the human condition notwithstanding mechanical advancement. As society wrestles with the difficulties and valuable open doors introduced by arising advancements, the continuous .

Chapter 5

Ethical Dilemmas of Nanotechnology

Nanotechnology, the control of issue at the nanoscale, holds massive commitment for extraordinary progressions in different fields, from medication and hardware to materials science and energy. Nonetheless, with these extraordinary open doors come moral problems that request cautious thought. As nanotechnology keeps on propelling, researchers, policymakers, and society at large are faced with complex inquiries regarding the capable turn of events and sending of nanomaterials and gadgets.

One of the essential moral worries in nanotechnology spins around potential wellbeing gambles related with openness to designed nanomaterials. At the nanoscale, materials can show special properties, like expanded reactivity and adjusted poisonousness. This brings up issues about the wellbeing of nanomaterials in purchaser items, modern applications, and clinical mediations. Guaranteeing the dependable utilization of nanotechnology requires thorough exploration to grasp the likely dangers to human wellbeing and the climate, combined with the improvement of rules and guidelines to alleviate these dangers.

In the domain of medication, nanotechnology offers imaginative ways to deal with diagnostics, drug conveyance, and treatment. Nanoscale drug transporters, for instance, can upgrade the accuracy of medication conveyance, focusing on unambiguous cells or tissues while limiting incidental effects. Nonetheless, the moral contemplations encompassing the utilization of nanomedicine incorporate inquiries regarding informed assent, long haul security, and the impartial admittance to these high level treatments. Finding some kind of harmony between propelling clinical therapies and shielding patient prosperity requires straightforward correspondence, vigorous administrative systems, and progressing checking of nanomedical mediations.

Nanotechnology's applications in observation and security additionally present moral difficulties. The advancement of nanoscale sensors and gadgets with reconnaissance abilities raises worries about meddling checking, possible maltreatment of innovation, and infringement of protection. As legislatures and confidential substances investigate the utilization of nanoscale reconnaissance instruments, moral rules should be laid out to forestall unjustifiable attacks of individual security and safeguard individual opportunities.

Besides, the potential for accidental ecological results presents a huge moral situation in nanotechnology. The arrival of designed nanomaterials into the climate, whether through modern cycles or the utilization of purchaser items, brings up issues about the drawn out environmental effect.

Understanding how nanomaterials connect with environments, untamed life, and human populaces is vital for expecting and alleviating likely damage. The moral basic is to adjust the advantages of nanotechnology with a guarantee to natural supportability and the prudent guideline.

In the work environment, the moral elements of nanotechnology become articulated with regards to word related wellbeing and security. As nanomaterials find applications in assembling and industry, the potential for laborer openness increments. Tending to this moral predicament requires the foundation of powerful security conventions, laborer preparing programs, and continuous exploration to comprehend the dangers related with word related openness to nanomaterials. Adjusting the quest for mechanical development with the obligation to safeguard the prosperity of laborers is fundamental for cultivating a capable nanotechnology industry.

Protected innovation and admittance to nanotechnology likewise raise moral contemplations. The improvement of new nanotechnologies frequently includes critical interests in innovative work. The subject of who benefits from these headways and who controls admittance to nanotechnology turns into an issue of moral concern. Finding some kind of harmony between boosting development through licensed innovation insurance and guaranteeing fair admittance to the advantages of nanotechnology for the more extensive worldwide local area is an intricate test that requires global coordinated effort and moral initiative.

In the field of energy, nanotechnology holds guarantee for more proficient energy creation, stockpiling, and usage. Nonetheless, moral predicaments emerge with regards to energy conveyance, asset assignment, and the potential for worsening existing social and monetary abberations. Guaranteeing that nanotechnology adds to maintainable and fair energy arrangements requires an all encompassing moral methodology that considers the more extensive cultural ramifications of energy innovations at the nanoscale.

Nanotechnology's combination with data innovation brings about moral worries connected with information security and digital dangers. The improvement of nanoscale sensors and gadgets for information capacity and correspondence presents new weaknesses that could be taken advantage of for noxious purposes. Defending against the abuse of nanotechnology in the domain of data security requests moral contemplations that focus on the assurance of delicate information and the anticipation of unapproved access.

The worldwide idea of nanotechnology innovative work additionally acquaints moral difficulties related with global joint effort, administration, and the capable sharing of information. As countries seek after progressions in nanotechnology, questions emerge about the evenhanded dissemination of advantages, the potential for double use applications with military ramifications, and the requirement for global collaboration to address shared difficulties.

Moral structures that advance straightforwardness, joint effort, and the dependable sharing of information are fundamental for encouraging a worldwide nanotechnology local area that focuses on the benefit of everyone.

Moral contemplations in nanotechnology are not restricted to logical and specialized spaces; they stretch out to public discernment and commitment. Really imparting the expected advantages and dangers of nanotechnology to general society is significant for building trust and cultivating informed independent direction. Tending to public worries and consolidating different viewpoints in the turn of events and administration of nanotechnology are moral goals that add to the mindful headway of the field.

The idea of "nanoethics" has arisen as a multidisciplinary field committed to investigating the moral ramifications of nanotechnology. Researchers, ethicists, and policymakers participate in conversations to foster structures that guide dependable exploration and advancement in nanotechnology. This incorporates resolving issues of straightforwardness, responsibility, value, and supportability, determined to guarantee that nanotechnology lines up with cultural qualities and goals.

One essential moral rule in nanotechnology is the preparatory guideline. As nanotechnology advances, it is fundamental to take on a careful and proactive methodology, recognizing the potential dangers even without any indisputable proof. The prudent guideline underscores the need to make a preventive move to stay away from hurt, especially while managing novel innovations where vulnerabilities exist.

Institutional oversight and administration systems assume a vital part in tending to moral predicaments in nanotechnology. Administrative bodies, research foundations, and expert associations should team up to lay out clear rules, sets of principles, and norms for moral direct in nanotechnology exploration and application. These components give a system to mindful independent direction, guaranteeing that moral contemplations are coordinated into each phase of nanotechnology improvement.

Instructing the up and coming age of researchers, designers, and policymakers on the moral elements of nanotechnology is fundamental for encouraging a culture of liability and responsibility. Coordinating morals schooling into nanotechnology educational programs assists future experts with exploring the moral difficulties they might experience in their vocations. It likewise ingrains a feeling of moral mindfulness and obligation that stretches out past specialized skill.

All in all, the moral problems of nanotechnology highlight the requirement for an all encompassing and proactive way to deal with mindful examination and development. As nanotechnology proceeds to develop and track down applications in different fields, from medication and energy to data innovation and assembling, moral contemplations should stay key to dynamic cycles.

A cooperative exertion among researchers, policymakers, ethicists, and general society is fundamental for creating moral structures that guide the capable turn of events and use of nanotechnology, guaranteeing that its advantages line up with cultural qualities and goals while limiting expected chances.

5.1 The ethics of manipulating matter at the nanoscale

The control of issue at the nanoscale, known as nanotechnology, addresses an outskirts of logical development with significant moral ramifications. As researchers dive into the domain of nanoscale materials and gadgets, moral contemplations become progressively basic. The novel properties and likely utilizations of nanotechnology bring up complex issues about security, natural effect, protection, and the more extensive cultural ramifications of controlling matter at such brief scale.

One of the essential moral worries in nanotechnology spins around the likely dangers to human wellbeing related with openness to designed nanomaterials. At the nanoscale, materials can show novel properties, and their way of behaving may contrast fundamentally from bigger scope partners. This brings up issues about the wellbeing of nanomaterials utilized in purchaser items, modern cycles, and clinical applications. Guaranteeing the dependable turn of events and utilization of nanotechnology requires thorough examination to comprehend the potential wellbeing chances and the foundation of rules and guidelines to moderate these dangers.

In the field of medication, nanotechnology offers noteworthy open doors for diagnostics, drug conveyance, and helpful mediations. Nanoscale drug transporters, for example, can upgrade the accuracy of medication conveyance, focusing on unambiguous cells or tissues with exceptional precision. Be that as it may, the moral contemplations encompassing nanomedicine incorporate inquiries concerning informed assent, long haul security, and the evenhanded admittance to these high level treatments. Finding some kind of harmony between propelling clinical therapies and protecting patient prosperity requires straightforward correspondence, powerful administrative structures, and progressing observing of nanomedical mediations.

The likely natural effect of nanotechnology is another moral worry that warrants cautious thought. Designed nanomaterials delivered into the climate, whether through modern cycles or the utilization of shopper items, may present dangers to environments and human wellbeing. Understanding how nanomaterials cooperate with the climate, untamed life, and human populaces is vital for expecting and relieving possible mischief. The moral basic is to adjust the advantages of nanotechnology with a promise to ecological supportability and the preparatory standard.

Protection and security concerns arise as critical moral contemplations with regards to nanotechnology. The improvement of nanoscale sensors and gadgets with reconnaissance capacities brings up issues about meddling observing, expected mal-treatment of innovation, and infringement of protection.

As nanotechnology merges with data innovation, the moral difficulties connected with information security, digital dangers, and the potential for unapproved observation become articulated. Shielding against the abuse of nanotechnology in the domain of data security requests moral contemplations that focus on the assurance of touchy information and the avoidance of unjustifiable interruptions.

In the work environment, word related wellbeing and security present moral situations with regards to nanotechnology. As nanomaterials find applications in assembling and industry, the potential for laborer openness increments. Tending to this moral concern requires the foundation of vigorous security conventions, laborer preparing programs, and continuous exploration to comprehend the dangers related with word related openness to nanomaterials. Adjusting the quest for mechanical de-velopment with the obligation to safeguard the prosperity of laborers is fundamental for cultivating a dependable nanotechnology industry.

The worldwide idea of nanotechnology innovative work acquaints moral difficulties related with global cooperation, administration, and the dependable sharing of infor-mation. As countries seek after headways in nanotechnology, questions emerge about the impartial dissemination of advantages, the potential for double use applications with military ramifications, and the requirement for global collaboration to address shared difficulties. Moral structures that advance straightforwardness, coordinated effort, and the dependable sharing of information are fundamental for cultivating a worldwide nanotechnology local area that focuses on the benefit of all.

Licensed innovation and admittance to nanotechnology additionally raise moral contemplations. The advancement of new nanotechnologies frequently includes criti-cal interests in innovative work. The subject of who benefits from these progressions and who controls admittance to nanotechnology turns into an issue of moral con-cern. Finding some kind of harmony between boosting development through licensed innovation security and guaranteeing evenhanded admittance to the advantages of nanotechnology for the more extensive worldwide local area is a complicated test that requires global cooperation and moral initiative.

The idea of "nanoethics" has arisen as a multidisciplinary field committed to investigating the moral ramifications of nanotechnology. Researchers, ethicists, and policymakers participate in conversations to foster structures that guide dependable exploration and development in nanotechnology. This incorporates resolving issues of straightforwardness, responsibility, value, and maintainability, determined to guaran-tee that nanotechnology lines up with cultural qualities and desires.

One major moral guideline in nanotechnology is the preparatory rule. As nano-technology advances, it is fundamental to take on a wary and proactive methodology, recognizing the potential dangers even without any indisputable proof.

The preparatory guideline accentuates the need to make a preventive move to stay away from hurt, especially while managing novel innovations where vulnerabilities exist.

Institutional oversight and administration components assume a significant part in tending to moral issues in nanotechnology. Administrative bodies, research foundations, and expert associations should team up to lay out clear rules, implicit sets of principles, and norms for moral lead in nanotechnology exploration and application. These instruments give a structure to dependable direction, guaranteeing that moral contemplations are incorporated into each phase of nanotechnology improvement.

Instructing the up and coming age of researchers, specialists, and policymakers on the moral elements of nanotechnology is fundamental for cultivating a culture of liability and responsibility. Coordinating morals training into nanotechnology educational plans assists future experts with exploring the moral difficulties they might experience in their vocations. It likewise ingrains a feeling of moral mindfulness and obligation that reaches out past specialized mastery.

Public discernment and commitment assume a urgent part in molding the moral scene of nanotechnology. Actually conveying the expected advantages and dangers of nanotechnology to general society is essential for building trust and cultivating informed independent direction. Tending to public worries and consolidating assorted viewpoints in the turn of events and administration of nanotechnology are moral goals that add to the capable progression of the field.

All in all, the moral predicaments of controlling matter at the nanoscale highlight the requirement for a comprehensive and proactive way to deal with capable examination and development. As nanotechnology proceeds to develop and track down applications in different fields, from medication and energy to data innovation and assembling, moral contemplations should stay vital to dynamic cycles. A cooperative exertion among researchers, policymakers, ethicists, and the general population is fundamental for creating moral systems that guide the mindful turn of events and utilization of nanotechnology, guaranteeing that its advantages line up with cultural qualities and yearnings while limiting likely dangers. The moral components of nanotechnology address a complex and developing scene, requesting continuous discourse and commitment to explore the difficulties and open doors introduced by this extraordinary field of logical request.

5.2 Balancing potential benefits and risks

Adjusting likely advantages and dangers is a principal challenge across different spaces of human undertaking, from mechanical development to public strategy and medical care. Striking the right harmony between boosting positive results and limiting potential unfortunate results is an intricate undertaking that requires cautious thought, moral investigation, and a guarantee to dependable direction. In this investigation, we will dive into various settings, including innovation, medical services, and ecological stewardship, to grasp the multi-layered nature of adjusting expected advantages and dangers.

Innovation and Advancement:

In the domain of innovation and development, the quest for progress frequently accompanies the intrinsic test of dealing with the possible advantages and dangers that new headways bring. Innovations, like man-made brainpower (artificial intelligence), biotechnology, and nanotechnology, hold huge commitment for changing businesses and working on human prosperity. Notwithstanding, they additionally raise moral worries and potential dangers that require insightful thought.

Take simulated intelligence, for instance. The possible advantages of man-made intelligence are huge, going from further developed proficiency in different areas to forward leaps in clinical diagnostics. Nonetheless, the dangers incorporate work dislodging, moral issues connected with algorithmic predisposition, and worries about the likely abuse of artificial intelligence in reconnaissance and direction. Finding some kind of harmony includes executing powerful moral rules, cultivating straightforwardness in computer based intelligence calculations, and guaranteeing that the advantages are appropriated impartially across society.

Essentially, the area of biotechnology offers progressive prospects, like quality altering for clinical medicines and the advancement of hereditarily adjusted crops for food security. Notwithstanding, moral worries about unseen side-effects, the potential for creator infants, and ecological effects require a cautious assessment of the dangers related with these innovations. Adjusting the likely advantages and dangers implies executing severe administrative structures, participating openly talk, and proactively tending to moral contemplations.

In the domain of nanotechnology, where materials are controlled at the nanoscale, potential advantages remember leap forwards for medication, energy, and materials science. Be that as it may, the dangers, for example, ecological effect and wellbeing concerns, require a mindful methodology. Finding some kind of harmony includes thorough examination on the wellbeing of nanomaterials, the advancement of moral rules, and proactive measures to moderate possible dangers.

Medical care and Clinical Mediations:

Adjusting likely advantages and dangers is especially urgent in medical care and clinical mediations, where choices straightforwardly influence people's prosperity. Clinical progressions, like novel medicines, quality treatments, and accuracy medication, offer phenomenal opportunities for working on tolerant results. In any case, moral problems emerge concerning issues of informed assent, admittance to medicines, and the drawn out impacts of mediations.

For example, quality altering advances like CRISPR-Cas9 hold the possibility to treat hereditary issues by exactly changing DNA. While this presents a progressive way to deal with medication, moral contemplations incorporate the potential for unseen side-effects, the heritability of hereditary changes, and the impartial admittance to these medicines. Finding some kind of harmony includes thorough clinical testing, straightforward correspondence with patients, and moral systems that guide the dependable utilization of quality altering advances.

With regards to drugs, the advancement of new medications offers the potential for further developed medicines and upgraded patient results. Nonetheless, the dangers incorporate unanticipated secondary effects, long haul wellbeing suggestions, and issues connected with drug estimating and availability. Adjusting expected advantages and dangers in the drug business requires severe administrative oversight, straightforward valuing models, and endeavors to guarantee that life-saving meds are available to those out of luck.

The continuous worldwide reaction to wellbeing emergencies, like the Coronavirus pandemic, highlights the significance of adjusting possible advantages and dangers in general wellbeing mediations. The fast turn of events and conveyance of immunizations, for example, offer expect controlling the spread of the infection and forestalling extreme ailment. Nonetheless, contemplations connected with antibody wellbeing, circulation value, and public trust should be painstakingly made due. Finding some kind of harmony includes straightforward correspondence, tending to antibody reluctance through schooling, and guaranteeing that immunization crusades focus on weak populaces.

Natural Stewardship:

In the domain of ecological stewardship, the sensitive harmony between receiving the rewards of regular assets and alleviating natural dangers becomes evident. The abuse of regular assets, like petroleum derivatives, has powered monetary turn of events however has additionally prompted natural debasement, environmental change, and loss of biodiversity. Adjusting expected advantages and dangers in ecological direction is a worldwide test that requires global cooperation and reasonable practices.

The shift towards environmentally friendly power sources, for example, sun oriented and wind power, epitomizes the endeavor to adjust the advantages of clean energy with the dangers related with petroleum derivative reliance. While sustainable power innovations offer a reasonable other option, contemplations about the natural effect of assembling, asset extraction, and waste administration should be tended to. Finding some kind of harmony includes putting resources into research for cleaner innovations, carrying out compelling strategies, and advancing a worldwide progress towards maintainable energy rehearses.

Also, the utilization of hereditarily adjusted life forms (GMOs) in horticulture brings up issues about adjusting likely advantages, for example, expanded crop yields and protection from bothers, with ecological and wellbeing gambles. Concerns incorporate the unseen side-effects of hereditary alterations, the effect on biological systems, and the potential for monoculture. Accomplishing an equilibrium includes vigorous testing and guideline of GMOs, as well as advancing agroecological rehearses that focus on biodiversity and supportability.

Moral Dynamic Systems:

In exploring the mind boggling territory of adjusting expected advantages and dangers, moral dynamic systems assume an essential part. These structures give core values to evaluating the ethical elements of decisions and activities.

One generally perceived moral structure is the principlism approach, which includes thinking about four key standards: independence, advantage, non-perniciousness, and equity.

Independence underlines regarding people's on the right track to settle on informed conclusions about their own lives, guaranteeing that they have the opportunity to pick and act as per their qualities. With regards to medical care, this guideline underlines the significance of informed assent, regarding patients' independence in clinical navigation.

Value centers around advancing prosperity and augmenting benefits. In medical services, this includes endeavoring to give the most ideal results to patients. In any case, it additionally requires cautious thought of possible dangers and guaranteeing that mediations line up with patients' qualities and inclinations.

Non-perniciousness highlights the commitment to cause no damage. That's what this guideline perceives, even chasing benefits, the evasion of mischief is principal. It implies a promise to limiting dangers and relieving expected unfortunate results in direction.

Equity underscores decency and value, guaranteeing that the dispersion of advantages and weights is simply and fair. In medical care, this standard calls for fair admittance to clinical therapies, tending to wellbeing variations, and taking into account the more extensive cultural effect of medical services choices.

Notwithstanding principlism, other moral structures, like consequentialism and deontology, offer alternate points of view on moral independent direction. Consequentialism assesses activities in light of their results, holding back nothing generally great. Deontology, then again, underlines adherence to moral standards and obligations, no matter what the results.

Applying moral dynamic structures includes a thorough investigation of the expected advantages and dangers, taking into account the specific situation, partners included, and the more extensive cultural effect. It requires a continuous obligation to reflection, straightforwardness, and responsiveness to evolving conditions.

Straightforwardness and Partner Commitment:

Straightforwardness and partner commitment are basic parts of mindful decision-production while adjusting possible advantages and dangers. Open correspondence guarantees that pertinent data is available to all partners, cultivating trust and considering informed direction. With regards to mechanical advancement, straightforwardness includes revealing data about the turn of events, security testing, and potential dangers related with new innovations.

Partner commitment goes past straightforwardness to effectively include the people who might be impacted by choices in the dynamic cycle. In medical services, this remembers drawing in patients for conversations about therapy choices, paying attention to their interests, and regarding their inclinations. In ecological direction, partners might incorporate nearby networks, native gatherings, and natural supporters whose viewpoints add to a more extensive comprehension of possible advantages and dangers.

5.3 The need for ethical guidelines and responsible research

The quick speed of mechanical headway and logical exploration has introduced exceptional open doors and difficulties. As society wanders into unfamiliar domains, the requirement for moral rules and capable exploration rehearses turns out to be progressively vital. Whether in the fields of man-made brainpower, biotechnology, or ecological science, moral contemplations assume a pivotal part in molding the direction of development and guaranteeing that progress lines up with cultural qualities and moral standards.

Man-made reasoning (computer based intelligence) and Moral Contemplations:

Man-made reasoning, with its ability for learning, direction, and independent activity, brings up significant moral issues that request cautious examination. As man-made intelligence frameworks become more coordinated into day to day existence, from medical services diagnostics to independent vehicles, the requirement for moral rules becomes apparent.

One moral worry in computer based intelligence spins around straightforwardness and responsibility. As computer based intelligence calculations go with choices that influence people and networks, understanding the thinking behind those choices becomes critical. Moral rules ought to underscore straightforwardness in man-made intelligence frameworks, guaranteeing that designers and clients can grasp the dynamic cycles and consider the innovation responsible for its activities.

Predisposition in man-made intelligence calculations is another basic moral thought. On the off chance that man-made intelligence frameworks are prepared on one-sided datasets, they might sustain and intensify existing cultural inclinations. Mindful exploration in man-made intelligence requires the recognizable proof and alleviation of predispositions, advancing reasonableness and value in algorithmic direction. Moral rules ought to highlight the significance of tending to predisposition and advancing inclusivity in artificial intelligence improvement.

Protection is a focal moral worry in the time of man-made intelligence, where huge measures of individual information are gathered and handled. Finding some kind of harmony between the advantages of information driven advancements and the assurance of individual security is vital. Moral rules ought to focus on the capable treatment of information, informed assent, and powerful safety efforts to protect people's security in the simulated intelligence scene.

Independent weapons frameworks present a one of a kind moral test, bringing up issues about the profound quality of designating life-and-demise choices to machines. The turn of events and utilization of such frameworks require cautious thought of the possible outcomes and moral ramifications. Mindful exploration in simulated intelligence includes assessing the cultural effect of independent weapons and laying out rules to forestall the abuse of artificial intelligence in manners that disregard common liberties and global regulation.

Biotechnology and Moral Contemplations:

Biotechnology, enveloping fields like quality altering, manufactured science, and cloning, presents moral difficulties at the crossing point of science, medication, and morals. As researchers gain remarkable abilities to control living creatures, the requirement for moral rules and dependable examination rehearses becomes basic.

Quality altering advances, especially CRISPR-Cas9, offer the possibility to treat hereditary problems and improve human abilities. Nonetheless, the moral contemplations encompassing germline altering, where changes are heritable and influence people in the future, bring up issues about the potentially negative results and long haul influence on the human genetic supply. Moral rules ought to depict limits for germline altering, taking into account the possible dangers and cultural ramifications.

In the domain of engineered science, the making of fake living things and the alteration of existing creatures present moral problems. Capable examination includes expecting the natural effect of engineered living beings, surveying likely potentially negative results, and laying out shields to forestall environmental interruptions. Moral rules ought to direct scientists in thinking about the more extensive ramifications of their work on biological systems and biodiversity.

Cloning, both regenerative and helpful, raises moral worries connected with the control of life and the potential for double-dealing. Mindful exploration in cloning includes cautious thought of the moral ramifications for cloned people and the cultural ramifications of cloning innovation. Moral rules ought to resolve issues of assent, independence, and the government assistance of cloned living beings.

The area of biotechnology additionally converges with inquiries of human improvement, inciting moral contemplations about the ethical limits of controlling human capacities. Mindful exploration in this space requires a smart assessment of the expected advantages and dangers of human improvement advances, alongside moral rules that focus on individual prosperity, value, and cultural qualities.

Natural Science and Moral Contemplations:

Natural science, as mankind wrestles with environmental change, asset consumption, and biodiversity misfortune, highlights the requirement for moral rules to illuminate capable examination and reasonable practices. The effect of human exercises in the world requires a promise to moral contemplations in ecological science.

Environmental change, driven by human exercises like consuming non-renewable energy sources and deforestation, represents an existential danger to the planet. Moral rules in ecological science ought to advocate for the dependable utilization of normal assets, the decrease of ozone harming substance emanations, and the quest for maintainable energy choices. Specialists have an ethical commitment to add to arrangements that relieve environmental change and safeguard the prosperity of current and people in the future.

Biodiversity protection is one more moral basic in ecological science. The deficiency of species and biological systems because of environment annihilation, contamination, and overexploitation brings up moral issues about humankind's liability to safeguard the variety of life on The planet. Moral rules ought to stress the conservation of biodiversity, feasible land use rehearses, and the moral treatment of non-human species.

Asset the executives and assignment present moral difficulties despite expanding worldwide interest for limited assets. From water shortage to mineral extraction, capable exploration in ecological science requires moral contemplations that focus on fair appropriation, reasonable practices, and the security of weak networks. Moral rules ought to direct specialists in advancing ecological equity and guaranteeing that asset use lines up with standards of decency and value.

The Significance of Moral Rules:

Moral rules act as a compass for specialists, policymakers, and professionals, giving a structure to exploring the intricacies of mechanical development, logical investigation, and natural stewardship. These rules offer a bunch of standards and values that guide direction, advance mindful lead, and guarantee that progressions in science and innovation line up with moral norms.

One vital part of moral rules is their job in advancing straightforwardness and responsibility. Clear rules guarantee that the moral contemplations of examination and development are made express, encouraging a culture of receptiveness and trust. Straightforward correspondence with the general population, partners, and administrative bodies improves responsibility, permitting society to consider analysts and establishments liable for the moral ramifications of their work.

Besides, moral rules give an establishment to tending to the possible dangers and potentially negative side-effects of exploration and innovative progressions. By illustrating moral contemplations, rules guide analysts in expecting and alleviating possible damages, whether in the advancement of computer based intelligence frameworks, the use of biotechnological mediations, or the investigation of natural arrangements.

Moral rules likewise assume a urgent part in cultivating worldwide coordinated effort and collaboration. In a globalized reality where logical exploration and mechanical headways rise above public boundaries, a common arrangement of moral standards becomes fundamental. Reliable rules assist with crossing over social and territorial contrasts, giving a typical moral system that works with coordinated effort in tending to worldwide difficulties.

For policymakers, moral rules offer a reason for creating guidelines and regulation that oversee research and innovative turn of events. By adjusting approaches to moral standards, states can establish a climate that supports dependable exploration, safeguards the public interest, and guarantees that cultural qualities are maintained chasing logical and innovative advancement.

Challenges and Advancing Nature of Moral Rules:

Regardless of their significance, moral rules face difficulties in staying up with the quickly developing scene of science and innovation. Arising fields, for example, neurotechnology, quantum figuring, and space investigation, present novel moral contemplations that may not be completely tended to by existing rules. The unique idea of mechanical advancement requests constant reflection and variation of moral systems to address new difficulties and intricacies.

One test is the possible hole between the improvement of innovations and the detailing of moral rules. As specialists push the limits of what is experimentally conceivable, moral contemplations might linger behind, causing circumstances where the moral ramifications of an innovation are not completely perceived or tended to until after it has been sent. Shutting this hole requires proactive endeavors to expect moral difficulties and integrate moral contemplations into the beginning phases of innovative work.

Chapter 6

The Unintended Consequences

The quest for progress and development has been a main thrust all through mankind's set of experiences, yielding headways in science, innovation, and society. In any case, entwined with these steps forward are the frequently unusual and potentially negative side-effects that emerge from our activities. Whether in the domain of mechanical development, social strategies, or ecological mediations, the law of potentially negative results fills in as an update that even benevolent activities can prompt unanticipated results. This investigation digs into different spaces where unseen side-effects play had a critical influence, molding the course of human undertakings.

Mechanical Advancement:

In the domain of mechanical development, the law of potentially negative side-effects is an unavoidable and complex power. Progressions in innovation have achieved extraordinary changes, upgrading our lives in manners unbelievable only years and years prior. However, woven into the texture of progress are unseen side-effects that can appear in unforeseen and now and again unfortunate ways.

Take the web, for instance. The formation of a worldwide associated network was imagined to work with correspondence, joint effort, and the sharing of data. While these objectives have been understood, the unseen side-effects have been significant. The ascent of digital dangers, online deception, and the disintegration of protection are unforeseen results that go with the advantages of an associated world. The fast multiplication of virtual entertainment stages, at first intended to cultivate associations, has led to worries about the spread of deception, polarization, and the intensification of outrageous perspectives.

Essentially, the coming of man-made reasoning (computer based intelligence) has presented another boondocks of potential outcomes and difficulties. Simulated intelligence frameworks, intended to increase human abilities and smooth out processes, have additionally raised moral worries and unseen side-effects. Issues of predisposition in calculations, the potential for work relocation, and the moral ramifications of independent navigation are difficulties that request cautious thought. Unseen side-effects in simulated intelligence feature the significance of mindful turn of events, straight-forwardness, and moral structures that expect and address possible dangers.

Social Strategies and Regulation:

Potentially negative results are not bound to the domain of innovation; they like-wise saturate social arrangements and regulation. Good natured endeavors to resolve cultural issues can prompt unforeseen results, affecting networks and people in man-ners that were not anticipated during the arrangement definition process.

One striking model is the "Battle on Medications" in the US. Started during the 1970s determined to control chronic drug use and dealing, this arrangement had po-tentially negative side-effects that lopsidedly impacted underestimated networks. The accentuation on corrective measures and mass imprisonment brought about a unique effect on minority populaces, fueling social imbalances and adding to the propagation of a pattern of neediness and wrongdoing.

Essentially, government assistance change arrangements pointed toward decreasing reliance on open help have had potentially negative results. While the expectation was to support independence, a few changes prompted expanded difficulty for weak pop-ulaces. Stricter qualification prerequisites and time limits on help, while proposing to spur people to look for work, some of the time left families without a security net, bringing about pessimistic results for kids and minimized networks.

In the domain of schooling, state sanctioned testing was carried out determined to guarantee responsibility and working on instructive results. Notwithstanding, the unseen side-effects incorporate limiting the educational plan, instructing to the test, and cultivating a culture of high-stakes testing that can be impeding to the two under-studies and teachers. The accidental results highlight the intricacy of social strategies and the requirement for a nuanced comprehension of their possible effect on different networks.

Natural Mediations:

Ecological mediations, whether in light of environmental change or asset the board, can likewise yield unseen side-effects that shape biological systems and human social orders in unexpected ways. The mind boggling interconnectedness of normal frame-works and the intricacies of human-climate cooperations make foreseeing results a difficult undertaking.

The acquaintance of non-local species with control nuisances or upgrade horti-cultural efficiency is an exemplary illustration of potentially negative side-effects in natural mediations. While the goal might be to address explicit difficulties, the pre-sented species can upset nearby biological systems, outcompeting local species, and prompting natural lopsided characteristics. The results can incorporate biodiversity misfortune, modified environment elements, and unanticipated difficulties in dealing with the presented species.

Essentially, enormous scope framework projects intended to oversee water assets or forestall cataclysmic events can have accidental ecological and social repercussions.

Dams, developed for flood control or hydroelectric power age, can change waterway biological systems, influence fish populaces, and dislodge networks. The potentially negative results might incorporate soil disintegration, changes in water quality, and the deficiency of social and environmental variety.

Environmental change mediations, for example, geoengineering proposition to alleviate a worldwide temperature alteration, likewise raise worries about potentially negative side-effects. While the aim is to control climbing temperatures, the likely effects on weather conditions, precipitation, and biological systems are unsure and could prompt unanticipated difficulties. The mind boggling nature of Earth's environment framework features the requirement for wary and all around informed dynamic in ecological mediations.

Market Elements and Monetary Strategies:

Market elements and financial arrangements are not invulnerable to potentially negative results. Monetary choices, expected to spike development, soundness, or monetary advancement, can have sweeping impacts that reach out past the underlying objectives. The many-sided snare of cooperations inside worldwide economies enhances the potential for unseen side-effects.

The monetary liberation of the late twentieth 100 years, expected to advance financial development and development, added to the circumstances that prompted the 2008 worldwide monetary emergency. The potentially negative results incorporated the breakdown of major monetary organizations, a serious financial slump, and far reaching joblessness. The emergency uncovered the delicacy of complicated monetary frameworks and the requirement for administrative systems that expect and alleviate likely dangers.

Likewise, money related strategies, like low-financing costs and quantitative facilitating, carried out because of monetary slumps, can have unseen side-effects. While these actions plan to animate monetary action, they might add to resource bubbles, pay disparity, and twists in monetary business sectors. The accidental results highlight the difficulties of exploring the intricate elements of worldwide economies.

Exchange arrangements, intended to cultivate global collaboration and financial development, can likewise yield potentially negative results. The rethinking of blue collar positions to cheaper districts, while expecting to lessen creation costs, can add to work uprooting and financial differences in significant expense areas. The unseen side-effects feature the requirement for an exhaustive comprehension of the social and monetary ramifications of exchange strategies.

Medical care Mediations:

In the domain of medical care, mediations and clinical progressions can prompt potentially negative side-effects that influence patient results, general wellbeing, and the medical services framework overall. Clinical medicines, drugs, and general wellbeing drives, while intended to further develop wellbeing results, may have unexpected impacts that become obvious solely after broad execution.

One model is the potentially negative results of anti-microbial use. The advancement of anti-microbials upset medication, saving incalculable lives by treating bacterial diseases. Be that as it may, the boundless and at times unpredictable utilization of anti-toxins has prompted the rise of anti-toxin safe microscopic organisms.

The potentially negative side-effect represents a critical danger to worldwide general wellbeing, requiring a reconsideration of anti-toxin recommending rehearses and the improvement of elective treatment procedures.

Immunization programs, intended to forestall the spread of irresistible infections, have likewise confronted potentially negative side-effects. At times, immunization reluctance has arisen because of deception, prompting flare-ups of preventable infections. The potentially negative results highlight the significance of powerful correspondence, state funded schooling, and addressing the cultural variables that add to immunization reluctance.

The utilization of electronic wellbeing records (EHRs) in medical services was expected to smooth out understanding consideration, further develop coordination among medical care suppliers, and upgrade the general effectiveness of the medical services framework. In any case, the boundless reception of EHRs has brought unseen side-effects, including worries about information security, protection breaks, and the potential for electronic records to be utilized for purposes past persistent consideration. Adjusting the advantages of advanced wellbeing innovations with moral contemplations and protection shields stays a continuous test.

Exploring Potentially negative results:

The predominance of potentially negative side-effects across different spaces highlights the requirement for a smart and versatile way to deal with navigation. While it could be trying to foresee each result, there are techniques and rules that can assist with moderating potentially negative side-effects and cultivate a stronger and responsive way to deal with progress.

1. **Frameworks Thinking:**

   Embracing a frameworks thinking approach is vital for figuring out the interconnectedness of factors inside complex frameworks. As opposed to zeroing in exclusively on detached parts or prompt results, frameworks thinking includes considering the more extensive setting and the potential far reaching influences of mediations. This all encompassing point of view assists chiefs with guessing how changes in a single piece of the framework might prompt unseen side-effects in different regions.

2. **Situation Arranging:**

   Situation arranging includes imagining different likely prospects and evaluating the potential outcomes of various strategies. By taking into account various situations, leaders can distinguish possible potentially negative side-effects and foster techniques to moderate or adjust to them. Situation arranging is especially significant in circumstances where vulnerabilities and intricacies make anticipating results testing.

3. **Moral Contemplations:**

Implanting moral contemplations in dynamic cycles can assist with directing activities that line up with cultural qualities and standards. Moral systems give an establishment to assessing the possible outcomes of mediations and surveying their effect on different partners.

Taking into account the moral ramifications of choices guarantees that potentially negative results are weighed against moral and social guidelines.

4. **Constant Observing and Assessment:**

Continuous observing and assessment of intercessions are fundamental for identifying and answering potentially negative side-effects as they arise. Normal evaluations permit chiefs to change systems, execute restorative measures, and gain from the results of mediations. This iterative interaction adds to a more versatile and responsive way to deal with complex difficulties.

5. **Partner Commitment:**

Counting assorted points of view through partner commitment can give important experiences into the expected results of choices. Partners, addressing networks, specialists, and impacted parties, can contribute one of a kind viewpoints and feature contemplations that might not have been clear during the dynamic cycle. Including partners cultivates straightforwardness, responsibility, and a more complete comprehension of possible effects.

6. **Preparatory Rule:**

The preparatory rule proposes making a preventive move even with vulnerability, particularly when there is a gamble of serious or irreversible mischief. While it doesn't kill vulnerability, the preparatory guideline advocates for a wary way to deal with direction, especially in circumstances where the potential results are not completely perceived. Embracing the preparatory rule can help forestall or limit potentially negative results when a lot is on the line.

7. **Interdisciplinary Coordinated effort:**

Coordinated effort among different trains and main subject areas improves the aggregate comprehension of mind boggling difficulties. Uniting specialists from different spaces cultivates a more extensive evaluation of expected results and works with the improvement of interdisciplinary arrangements. Interdisciplinary joint effort evades siloed thinking and urges an all encompassing way to deal with direction.

8. **Public Commitment and Training:**

Drawing in general society in dynamic cycles and giving schooling about potential results cultivates a more educated and enabled populace. Public mindfulness can add to dependable ways of behaving, informed decisions, and a superior comprehension of the possible effects of intercessions. Informed public commitment likewise goes about as a keep an eye on chiefs, advancing responsibility and moral administration.

The law of potentially negative results fills in as a steady sign of the mind boggling and interconnected nature of human undertakings. From mechanical development and social strategies to ecological mediations and monetary choices, the repercussions of our activities frequently reach out past our underlying expectations.

Exploring the intricacies of unseen side-effects requires a promise to moral direction, frameworks thinking, and persistent transformation.

As society wrestles with uncommon difficulties and valuable open doors, the capacity to expect, screen, and answer potentially negative side-effects turns out to be progressively critical. Embracing a mentality that recognizes the intrinsic vulnerabilities of mind boggling frameworks, values moral contemplations, and effectively connects with different viewpoints is fundamental for cultivating flexibility and moderating the likely adverse consequences of our activities.

While what's in store stays unsure, and potentially negative results are unavoidable, the quest for progress can be directed by rules that focus on the prosperity of people, networks, and the planet. By embracing a proactive and versatile way to deal with direction, we can endeavor to limit potentially negative side-effects, gain from our encounters, and add to an additional maintainable and impartial world.

6.1 Scenarios that could lead to rogue nanobots

The idea of maverick nanobots, infinitesimal robots working freely and possibly inflicting any kind of damage, has for some time been a staple of sci-fi. Nonetheless, as headways in nanotechnology keep on advancing, the chance of certifiable situations that could prompt rebel nanobots merits cautious thought. This investigation dives into likely situations, both speculative and grounded in current logical comprehension, that could add to the rise of rebel nanobots.

1. **Unseen side-effects of Clinical Nanotechnology:**

   One road through which maverick nanobots could arise includes unseen side-effects in the field of clinical nanotechnology. The improvement of nanobots for clinical purposes, for example, designated drug conveyance or painless diagnostics, holds enormous commitment for upsetting medical care. In any case, the intrinsic intricacy of nanoscale frameworks presents the gamble of potentially negative side-effects that could prompt the rise of rebel nanobots.

   Chasing after upgrading clinical medicines, scientists might plan nanobots with refined abilities to explore through the human body, target explicit cells, and convey helpful payloads. While possibly not fastidiously designed and controlled, these nanobots could go through accidental transformations or glitches, possibly prompting erratic way of behaving. Such glitches could result in nanobots going astray from their planned errands, hurting sound cells or tissues.

   Moreover, issues of safety in clinical nanotechnology could add to the maverick way of behaving of nanobots. On the off chance that these nanobots are some-what controlled or modified remotely, they might be defenseless to hacking or unapproved access. Pernicious entertainers with the information and goal to take advantage of weaknesses could oversee the nanobots, diverting them for unsafe purposes, like designated assaults inside the human body or the arrival of poisonous substances.

2. **Military Applications and Heightening:**

One more potential situation includes the advancement of nanobots for military applications. States and military elements overall are putting resources into exploration to tackle the capacities of nanotechnology for purposes going from reconnaissance to designated mediations. While the essential objective might be to acquire a competitive edge, the unseen side-effects of such military applications could prompt the rise of maverick nanobots.

In a situation where nanobots are weaponized for military purposes, unseen side-effects could emerge during sending or battle circumstances. Nanobots intended for observation, knowledge assembling, or even designated assaults on adversary warriors could glitch or be dependent upon flighty natural variables. This could result in these nanobots acting autonomously, digressing from their customized mandates, and actually hurting regular folks or associated powers.

Moreover, the heightening of military uses of nanobots could prompt a situation where contending countries or substances participate in a mechanical weapons contest. The race to grow progressively modern and strong nanobots could out-perform the capacity to successfully control and direct their way of behaving. In this climate, the development of rebel nanobots turns into a possible outcome of the quest for military predominance through nanotechnology.

3. **Nanobot-based Cyberattacks:**

As society turns out to be more interconnected through the Web of Things (IoT) and savvy innovations, the potential for nanobot-based cyberattacks arises as an unsettling situation. Nanobots intended for different applications, includ-ing clinical medicines or ecological observing, might be associated with networks for controller and checking. In case of a cyberattack, these nanobots could be taken advantage of to complete deplorable acts.

A complex cyberattack focusing on nanobots could control their programming, change their way of behaving, or render them non-useful. This situation turns out to be particularly basic if the nanobots are engaged with pivotal under-takings, like medication conveyance inside the human body or natural cleanup endeavors. A fruitful cyberattack could prompt the arrival of destructive sub-stances, disturbance of clinical medicines, or the split the difference of natural security measures.

Also, the joining of nanobots into basic framework, like water treatment offices or energy lattices, could give open doors to malignant entertainers to take advantage of weaknesses. A cyberattack focusing on nanobots in these frameworks could prompt pollution of water supplies, disturbance of energy dissemination, or other devastating outcomes.

4. **Moral Contemplations and Accidental Purposes:**

The moral contemplations encompassing nanotechnology likewise present an expected pathway to the development of maverick nanobots. As researchers and specialists investigate the moral components of nanotechnology, the accidental purposes of this innovation might turn into a wellspring of concern. For instance, the advancement of nanobots for observation or information assortment, even with at first altruistic expectations, could be co-selected untrustworthy purposes.

In the event that nanobots are intended to assemble information about people, their way of behaving, or their wellbeing, there is a gamble that these capacities could be abused for protection encroachments or unapproved reconnaissance. In a situation where administrative structures are deficient or neglect to stay up with mechanical progressions, the moral contemplations encompassing the accidental purposes of nanobots could add to their rebel conduct.

Besides, the potential for corporate interests to drive nanotechnology applications raises worries about unseen side-effects. Organizations creating nanobots for business purposes, for example, designated promoting or shopper observing, may focus on benefit over moral contemplations. This benefit driven approach could prompt the arrangement of nanobots with potentially negative side-effects, like the unapproved assortment of touchy individual data or the control of shopper conduct.

5. **Natural Delivery and Environmental Effect:**

A situation that could prompt the development of rebel nanobots includes their incidental delivery into the climate. As nanotechnology applications extend, the potential for incidental deliveries during assembling, transportation, or removal processes turns into a critical concern. Once delivered into the climate, nanobots could associate with biological systems in manners that were not anticipated during their plan and advancement.

In case of an ecological delivery, nanobots intended for clinical medicines or modern applications could affect biological systems, possibly hurting plant and creature life. The unseen side-effects might incorporate disturbances to the well established order of things, adjustments in soil piece, or accidental natural lopsided characteristics. Nanobots delivered into oceanic conditions, for example, could connect with marine life in unanticipated ways, influencing biodiversity and biological system wellbeing.

Furthermore, the ecological steadiness of nanobots raises worries about their drawn out influence. Nanobots intended for explicit errands inside the human body or modern cycles may not corrupt normally in the climate. Their gathering over the long run could prompt unseen side-effects, including the pollution of normal assets and biological systems.

Alleviating the Gamble of Rebel Nanobots:

As the investigation of nanotechnology proceeds and the potential situations prompting maverick nanobots become evident, endeavors to relieve these dangers and guarantee mindful improvement are basic. A few systems can be executed to limit the probability of rebel nanobots and address the potentially negative results related with their sending.

1. **Powerful Moral Rules and Guidelines:**
   Laying out complete moral rules and administrative systems for the turn of events and sending of nanobots is pivotal. These rules ought to envelop all parts of nanobot applications, from clinical purposes to military applications, and ought to focus on moral contemplations, wellbeing, and security. Administrative bodies should team up with researchers, ethicists, and different partners to persistently evaluate and refresh these rules as the innovation develops.

2. **Security Conventions for Nanobots:**
   In situations where nanobots are somewhat controlled or remotely associated with networks, carrying out strong security conventions is fundamental. Encryption, confirmation systems, and secure correspondence channels can help shield nanobots from unapproved access and control. Furthermore, consolidating safeguard components and crisis closure strategies can give a layer of control in case of a security break.

3. **Straightforward Innovative work Practices:**
   Advancing straightforwardness in the innovative work of nanobots is fundamental for building public trust and guaranteeing dependable advancement. Specialists and associations associated with nanotechnology ought to impart transparently about the objectives, abilities, and potential dangers related with their work. Straightforward practices work with public mindfulness, informed direction, and the distinguishing proof of expected unseen side-effects.

4. **Global Cooperation and Administration:**

Given the worldwide idea of nanotechnology innovative work, global joint effort is significant. Laying out worldwide administration systems that work with participation, data sharing, and the improvement of all inclusive moral guidelines can add to capable nanobot advancement. Peaceful accords and coordinated efforts can assist with forestalling a cutthroat race that could think twice about and oversight.

6.2 Potential catalysts for catastrophic replication

The thought of disastrous replication, frequently connected with the speculative situation of "dim goo," has been a subject of conversation and worry in the domain of nanotechnology. The thought includes self-repeating nanobots multiplying wildly, consuming matter and possibly hurting. While this idea has its foundations in speculative sci-fi, investigating expected impetuses for devastating replication is fundamental in evaluating the dangers and executing shields as nanotechnology propels. This investigation considers different variables, both hypothetical and grounded in logical comprehension, that could go about as impetuses for devastating replication.

1. **Programming Mistakes and Glitches:**
   One of the major difficulties in nanotechnology, especially in the improvement of self-reproducing nanobots, lies in the complexities of programming and control. Programming mistakes, whether presented during the underlying plan stage or because of unanticipated communications, could act as an impetus for disastrous replication.

   In a situation where nanobots are modified to self-imitate with explicit imperatives and restrictions, a programming blunder could think twice about shields. A minor error or oversight could prompt uncontrolled replication, causing nanobots to overlook modified limitations and multiply quickly. This could bring about the accidental utilization of assets, natural lopsided characteristics, and possibly present dangers to living life forms.

   Furthermore, the potential for outer variables, like radiation or electromagnetic obstruction, to actuate glitches in nanobot programming raises concerns. Assuming these outer impacts disturb the control components or correspondence channels of self-reproducing nanobots, it could set off uncontrolled replication, prompting accidental and possibly devastating results.

2. **Developmental Variations and Potentially negative side-effects:**
   The idea of nanobots advancing and adjusting over the long run presents one more expected impetus for devastating replication. In a situation where nanobots are planned with the limit with regards to personal growth or variation to evolving conditions, unseen side-effects might emerge because of their developmental elements.

   In the event that nanobots have the capacity to go through hereditary changes or alterations in light of ecological upgrades, there is a gamble that these transformations could prompt unforeseen ways of behaving. Transformative cycles could lean toward attributes that improve replication productivity disregarding the more extensive outcomes. This could bring about a shift toward more forceful replication systems, possibly unbelievable the expected limits and prompting disastrous situations.

   Also, potentially negative results could rise up out of the associations between self-reproducing nanobots and the general climate. As nanobots adjust to take advantage of accessible assets, unanticipated natural interruptions might happen. The unseen side-effects of developmental variations highlight the requirement for thorough gamble appraisals and shields in the plan and arrangement of self-imitating nanobots.

3. **Absence of Regulation and Escapement:**
The actual regulation of nanobots is a basic thought to forestall accidental replication and possible disastrous situations. Deficient control measures, whether because of configuration defects, material weaknesses, or coincidental breaks, could act as an impetus for nanobot escapement and uncontrolled replication.

In the event that nanobots are intended for explicit conditions, like controlled research facility settings, and afterward delivered into the wild without adequate regulation, the gamble of accidental replication in uncontrolled conditions increments. Factors like breeze, water, or unplanned dispersal could add to nanobot escapement, prompting accidental cooperations with environments and uncontrolled replication.

Besides, the absence of safeguard systems or safeguard control techniques in case of breaks represents a huge gamble. Assuming that control frameworks fall flat, deliberately or inadvertently, nanobots may escape into the climate, possibly starting horrendous replication. Tending to the difficulties of control and escapement is essential to limiting the gamble related with the uncontrolled multiplication of self-repeating nanobots.

4. **Asset Contest and Accidental Biological Effect:**
Self-imitating nanobots, intended to use nearby assets for replication, could incidentally prompt asset rivalry and accidental environmental effect. In a situation where nanobots are modified to separate materials from the climate for replication, rivalry for fundamental assets might emerge, possibly hurting environments.

Assuming nanobots are brought into a climate with restricted assets, their uncontrolled replication could prompt the consumption of basic components important for the endurance of different creatures. This asset rivalry could bring about biological uneven characters, influencing biodiversity, soil creation, or other environment capabilities. The accidental natural effect of nanobots taking part in asset serious replication raises moral and ecological worries.

Furthermore, assuming nanobots are intended to use flighty or manufactured materials for replication, the potentially negative results of asset extraction and use might stretch out past biological contemplations. The consumption of explicit materials or the accidental arrival of results during replication could have extensive ramifications for businesses, supply chains, and worldwide economies.

5. **Accidental Cooperations with Living Creatures:**
The potential for self-imitating nanobots to connect with living organic entities presents one more element of chance. In the event that nanobots are intended to recreate inside a natural host for clinical or remedial purposes, accidental cooperations could prompt uncontrolled replication and potentially negative

results.

In a clinical setting, nanobots intended for designated drug conveyance inside the human body could confront difficulties connected with accidental collaborations with natural frameworks. In the event that these nanobots display startling ways of behaving, for example, expanded replication rates or adjusted focusing on components, they could think twice about expected health advantages and posture dangers to the host organic entity.

Additionally, if self-imitating nanobots are intended to associate with microbial networks in natural remediation endeavors, potentially negative results might emerge. The potential for nanobots to coincidentally affect advantageous microorganisms or upset biological equilibriums could bring about accidental replication and environmental aggravations.

6. **Absence of Guideline and Oversight:**

The shortfall of vigorous administrative structures and oversight components represents a huge gamble in the turn of events and organization of self-recreating nanobots. In the event that there is an absence of worldwide agreement on norms for nanotechnology, including wellbeing conventions, moral rules, and regulation measures, it could add to the rise of horrendous replication situations.

In a situation where nanobots are created and conveyed without satisfactory administrative examination, there might be deficient shields to forestall potentially negative results. The shortfall of state sanctioned testing conventions, moral contemplations, and exhaustive gamble evaluations could bring about the uncontrolled arrival of nanobots with the potential for disastrous replication.

Also, the absence of worldwide coordinated effort and data sharing systems might upset the capacity to address arising gambles expeditiously. Without an organized way to deal with guideline and oversight, individual drives in various districts might come up short on fundamental governing rules, improving the probability of potentially negative side-effects related with self-duplicating nanobots.

7. **Accidental Mix with Existing Advances:**

The mix of self-imitating nanobots with existing advancements could present unexpected difficulties and catalyze accidental replication situations. On the off chance that nanobots are intended to cooperate with other shrewd advancements, like the Web of Things (IoT) or man-made brainpower frameworks, the potential for unseen side-effects increments.

In a situation where nanobots are coordinated into complex mechanical biological systems, unexpected collaborations with different advances could prompt accidental replication. Issues like correspondence mistakes, programming weaknesses, or accidental input circles might arise, adding to uncontrolled multiplication of nanobots past the planned degree.

Furthermore, on the off chance that nanobots are intended to impart and facilitate with one another as a component of a bigger framework, the unseen side-effects of aggregate ways of behaving may turn into an impetus for devastating replication. Without complete testing and chance evaluations that record for the mix of nanobots with existing innovations, the potential for accidental situations stays a critical concern.

6.3 The global implications of a grey goo event

The idea of a "dark goo" occasion, portrayed by the uncontrolled replication of self-imitating nanobots consuming all matter in their way, conveys significant and expansive worldwide ramifications. While presently bound to the domains of speculative sci-fi, the likely development of a dim goo situation raises basic contemplations across different spaces, including ecological, monetary, moral, and international aspects. This investigation digs into the possible worldwide ramifications of a dark goo occasion and highlights the requirement for dependable turn of events and vigorous shields in the area of nanotechnology.

1. **Ecological Disaster:**

   A dark goo occasion would release a disastrous natural emergency, as self-recreating nanobots consume natural and inorganic matter the same. The uncontrolled replication of nanobots could prompt the exhaustion of fundamental assets, disturbance of biological systems, and irreversible harm to the regular habitat. As nanobots multiply, they would insatiably consume biomass, upsetting the fragile harmony between biological systems and causing flowing consequences for verdure.

   The environmental ramifications of a dim goo occasion reach out past prompt asset consumption. The far and wide annihilation of biodiversity, soil organization, and oceanic environments could prompt the breakdown of whole biological frameworks. The deficiency of key species, interruption of well established pecking orders, and change of normal territories would have persevering through outcomes, affecting the climate as well as the vocations of networks reliant upon sound environments.

2. **Monetary Interruption:**

   The worldwide monetary consequences of a dark goo occasion would be significant and complex. Enterprises depending on normal assets, like horticulture, ranger service, and mining, would confront prompt and serious interruptions. The uncontrolled replication of nanobots consuming unrefined components could prompt deficiencies, cost instability, and the breakdown of areas subject to these assets.

   Also, the assembling and innovation areas, which are fundamental to the worldwide economy, would be seriously influenced. Nanotechnology, while holding monstrous potential for development and monetary development, could confront a kickback and expanded examination. The feeling of dread toward unseen side-effects and the potential for a dark goo occasion could bring about a log jam or even an end in nanotechnology innovative work, influencing businesses going from medical care to gadgets.

Worldwide inventory chains would be helpless against the interruptions brought about by a dark goo occasion. As nanobots consume materials fundamental for assembling, the creation of products would be seriously hampered, prompting deficiencies and monetary misfortunes.

The interconnected idea of the worldwide economy implies that disturbances in a single locale could have flowing impacts, influencing organizations, exchange, and monetary business sectors around the world.

3. **Moral and Cultural Worries:**

   A dark goo occasion brings up significant moral issues about the mindful turn of events and organization of innovation. The potentially negative side-effects of self-duplicating nanobots consuming all matter feature the moral basic of focusing on security, risk evaluation, and adherence to moral rules in logical and mechanical undertakings.

   The moral contemplations reach out to inquiries of responsibility and obligation. In case of a dim goo situation, deciding culpability and tending to the outcomes would be mind boggling. The potential for unseen side-effects highlights the requirement for powerful moral structures, straightforwardness in research practices, and components for responsibility in the improvement of arising advances.

   Cultural confidence in science, innovation, and development could be fundamentally disintegrated in the outcome of a dim goo occasion. Public impression of the dangers related with trend setting innovations, especially nanotechnology, may move towards incredulity and watchfulness. Reconstructing public trust would require straightforward correspondence, moral administration, and a guarantee to gaining from the results of accidental occasions.

4. **International Effect:**

   The development of a dark goo occasion could have significant international ramifications, influencing relations among countries and impacting worldwide administration structures. In the event that a country or substance is seen as liable for the turn of events or sending of the nanobots prompting a dark goo situation, strategic pressures, and potential contentions could emerge.

   International contemplations would reach out to inquiries of obligation and risk. The absence of global agreement and administrative systems for nanotechnology could confuse endeavors to address the outcomes of a dark goo occasion. Composed worldwide reactions would be fundamental to contain and alleviate the effect, however the shortfall of laid out conventions could prompt difficulties in cooperation.

Besides, the international aftermath could appear as expanded guidelines and limitations on the turn of events and arrangement of arising advances. Countries could embrace defensive measures to protect against possible dangers, prompting a divided way to deal with mechanical progression. The opposition for mechanical strength could heighten, with countries trying to lay out administration in regions saw as more secure or less inclined to devastating occasions.

5. **Mechanical Stagnation and Anxiety toward Advancement:**

The event of a dim goo occasion would probably impart dread and mindfulness in regards to the quick progression of innovation. The anxiety toward unseen side-effects and the potential for devastating occasions could bring about a hesitance to embrace creative innovations, smothering advancement and blocking the advantages that capable mechanical progression could bring.

The phantom of a dark goo situation might prompt expanded administrative examination and public requests for rigid controls on arising innovations. States and administrative bodies might force limitations on innovative work to relieve apparent dangers, unintentionally hindering logical investigation and mechanical advancement.

The anxiety toward mechanical development could penetrate cultural perspectives, impacting popular assessment and molding social accounts. This could prompt a hesitance to embrace new innovations, even those with huge potential for positive effect. The outcomes of a dark goo occasion would probably create a long shaded area, impacting cultural perspectives towards logical and innovative advancement for a long time into the future.

6. **Worldwide Coordinated effort for Relief:**

Tending to the worldwide ramifications of a dim goo occasion requires global joint effort and participation. The interconnectedness of the cutting edge world requires a unified reaction to moderate the effect, contain the spread of nanobots, and foster systems for ecological remediation. Worldwide administration structures and cooperative endeavors would be pivotal in exploring the complicated difficulties presented by such an occasion.

Worldwide associations, like the Unified Countries, could assume a urgent part in organizing reactions and working with cooperation among countries. Laying out conventions for data sharing, asset designation, and emergency the board would be fundamental parts of a worldwide procedure to address the results of a dim goo occasion.

Research organizations, researchers, and specialists from around the world would have to pool their assets and information to foster successful countermeasures. Established researchers' capacity to share information, bits of knowledge, and mechanical arrangements would be instrumental in conceiving methodologies to contain and kill the nanobots liable for the devastating replication.

7. **Improvement of Worldwide Protections:**
The event of a dim goo occasion would highlight the criticalness of laying out vigorous worldwide shields for arising innovations, especially in the area of nanotechnology. The advancement of worldwide administrative structures, moral rules, and wellbeing conventions is fundamental to forestall potentially negative side-effects and guarantee mindful development.

Peaceful accords on the moral utilization of innovation and the execution of wellbeing measures could set norms for countries and elements engaged with mechanical innovative work. A worldwide obligation to moral practices, straightforwardness, and dependable administration would assist with building public trust and relieve the dangers related with arising innovations.

Furthermore, the improvement of safeguard systems and regulation techniques should be vital. Cooperative exploration endeavors ought to zero in on planning advances with worked in shields to forestall uncontrolled replication and relieve the results of any expected breakdown.

8. **Public Mindfulness and Training:**

Upgrading public mindfulness and training about the possible dangers and advantages of arising advancements is pivotal in planning social orders for the difficulties representing things to come. A very much educated public is better prepared to participate in conversations, consider chiefs responsible, and add to the moral administration of innovation.

Public mindfulness missions ought to plan to demystify complex logical ideas, advance comprehension of possible dangers, and encourage a feeling of shared liability regarding the moral improvement of innovation. Instructive drives could zero in on engaging people to go with informed choices, partake in moral conversations, and promoter for mindful mechanical practices.

Chapter 7

The Role of Regulation and Policy

In the unpredictable embroidered artwork of cultural association, guideline and strategy arise as the twist and weft, winding around together the texture of administration and request. These two points of support assume a crucial part in molding the elements of economies, protecting individual privileges, and guiding the direction of mechanical progressions. As the world plunges through the 21st hundred years, the meaning of vigorous administrative systems and informed approach choices turns out to be progressively evident.

At the core of the matter lies the sensitive harmony between individual opportunity and aggregate liability. The development of social orders has seen a persistent interchange between these two powers, with guideline and strategy going about as the referees of this sensitive balance. Fundamentally, they are the classified articulations of a general public's qualities and goals, offering a guide for exploring the intricacies of human cooperation.

Financial frameworks, as the motors pushing countries forward, stand as perfect representations of the multifaceted dance between guideline, strategy, and the undetectable hand of the market. In the beginning of free enterprise, free enterprise standards held influence, advocating negligible government mediation and confiding in the market to control itself. Be that as it may, the free quest for benefit frequently prompted manipulative practices, ecological corruption, and the centralization of abundance among the trivial few.

Perceiving the requirement for a more impartial dissemination of assets and the security of weak populaces, social orders all over the planet started to embrace administrative measures and extensive strategies. Work regulations were authorized to protect laborers' privileges, antitrust guidelines looked to forestall restraining infrastructures, and ecological arrangements pointed toward controlling the unfriendly effects of industrialization. These intercessions denoted a change in outlook, recognizing that unrestrained private enterprise could plant the seeds of its own obliteration.

The 2008 worldwide monetary emergency filled in as a distinct sign of the possible traps in monetary business sectors when left unrestrained. Legislatures mixed to execute administrative changes to support monetary foundations, safeguard customers, and forestall a repeat of such devastating occasions. The emergency highlighted the basic for a tweaked administrative contraption fit for expecting and relieving foundational gambles, finding some kind of harmony between market dynamism and solidness.

As innovation proceeds with its persevering walk, infiltrating each feature of human life, the administrative scene should adjust to the difficulties and open doors introduced by the computerized age. The coming of blockchain, man-made consciousness, and the Web of Things has introduced uncommon potential outcomes, however it has additionally raised worries about protection, security, and the moral ramifications of innovative headways.

In this state-of-the-art existence, policymakers wind up exploring unknown waters, entrusted with making guidelines that encourage development while protecting the public interest. The advanced domain is innately borderless, rising above conventional ideas of locale. Thusly, the test lies in making administrative systems that are both deft and universally organized, fit for tending to the transnational idea of computerized advancements.

Information protection remains at the front of these difficulties. In a time where individual data has turned into a significant ware, the requirement for powerful information security guidelines is fundamental. The Overall Information Security Guideline (GDPR) in the European Association fills in as a spearheading model, giving people more noteworthy command over their own information and forcing rigid prerequisites on organizations that handle such data. As different countries wrestle with comparable worries, the GDPR has set a benchmark for administrative drives looking to figure out some kind of harmony among development and security.

The ascent of man-made consciousness represents one more impressive test for controllers. As machines progressively take on dynamic jobs, inquiries of responsibility, straightforwardness, and predisposition come to the front. Policymakers should wrestle with characterizing the limits of computer based intelligence applications, guaranteeing that these advancements serve mankind as opposed to oppress it. Moral contemplations pose a potential threat in this space, requiring the definition of strategies that line up with cultural qualities and forestall the abuse of man-made intelligence for vindictive purposes.

While the computerized scene presents novel administrative difficulties, it additionally offers extraordinary open doors for improved effectiveness and inclusivity. Fintech, for example, has reformed the monetary area, democratizing admittance to monetary administrations and cultivating monetary consideration. Nonetheless, this quick development requires administrative structures that can adjust to the high speed nature of mechanical headways. Finding some kind of harmony expects controllers to draw in with industry partners, keeping up to date with improvements to guarantee that guidelines stay successful and important.

Natural worries, exacerbated by environmental change, have pushed administrative and strategy drives pointed toward alleviating the effect of human exercises in the world. The Paris Understanding, endorsed by countries all over the planet, addresses an aggregate obligation to checking worldwide temperature increase and progressing to a feasible future.

In any case, the viability of such arrangements relies on the execution of strong strategies that boost green innovations, punish natural debasement, and encourage a worldwide ethos of biological obligation.

In the domain of medical care, the Coronavirus pandemic plays highlighted the basic part of administrative readiness. The fast turn of events and sending of immunizations, while a victory of logical resourcefulness, brought up issues about the harmony among speed and wellbeing in administrative endorsements. The pandemic provoked a reexamination of administrative cycles, featuring the requirement for lithe systems that can speed up the endorsement of life-saving mediations without compromising wellbeing norms.

Instruction, as well, ends up at the convergence of guideline and strategy. As the conventional model of training goes through change through web based learning stages and computerized assets, controllers should wrestle with guaranteeing quality, availability, and value in instructive open doors. The Coronavirus pandemic sped up the reception of remote picking up, revealing insight into the computerized gap and provoking policymakers to resolve issues of web access and innovative education.

The common agreement among residents and the express, the basic bedrock of administration, is unpredictably attached to the viability of administrative and strategy structures. Trust in foundations dissolves when guidelines are seen as erratic, one-sided, or ineffectual. On the other hand, very much created strategies that address the requirements and goals of different populaces add to a feeling of social union and aggregate prosperity.

Be that as it may, the errand of creating and executing viable guidelines is no simple accomplishment. Policymakers should battle with the intricacies of human way of behaving, the steadily advancing scene of innovation, and the complex idea of worldwide difficulties. In addition, the potential for unseen side-effects poses a potential threat, as administrative mediations in a single space might have expanding influences across interconnected frameworks.

The job of administrative bodies stretches out past rule-production; they should likewise go about as watchful gatekeepers, adjusting to arising gambles and guaranteeing the authorization of laid out standards. The adequacy of guidelines pivots on their substance as well as on the limit with respect to requirement and the capacity to adjust to evolving conditions. An administrative system without any trace of teeth is similar to a compass without a needle — it might point in the correct bearing, however without the necessary resources to explore the territory, it misses the mark concerning its expected reason.

Chasing after administrative greatness, joint effort between general society and confidential areas is principal. Industry skill is essential in making guidelines that find some kind of harmony between cultivating advancement and protecting public government assistance.

Open discourse and straightforward correspondence among controllers and industry partners can assist with crossing over holes in understanding, guaranteeing that guidelines are powerful as well as intelligent of the real factors on the ground.

The worldwide idea of many difficulties, from environmental change to digital dangers, highlights the requirement for global joint effort in the domain of guideline and strategy. Transnational issues require transnational arrangements, requiring a blended methodology that rises above international limits. Associations, for example, the Unified Countries assume a critical part in working with collaboration and standard-setting, going about as discussions for countries to address shared difficulties on the whole.

The advancing idea of work and the gig economy present extra intricacies for controllers. Conventional work regulations, made in a period of stable business and clear boss representative connections, may battle to adjust to the liquid elements of contemporary work game plans. Policymakers should wrestle with issues of laborers' privileges, employer stability, and social security nets in a scene where the conventional ideas of work are going through a significant change.

Despite these difficulties, administrative sandboxes have arisen as trial spaces where new advancements and plans of action can be tried in a controlled climate. These sandboxes give a center ground, taking into consideration development without compromising administrative oversight. They act as pots for refining guidelines, empowering policymakers to notice this present reality ramifications of their choices before inescapable execution.

7.1 International efforts to regulate nanotechnology

Nanotechnology, the control of issue at the nuclear and sub-atomic scale, addresses a wilderness of logical and mechanical development with significant ramifications for different businesses. From medication to hardware, the utilizations of nanotechnology hold the commitment of extraordinary forward leaps. Nonetheless, likewise with any integral asset, the dependable and moral utilization of nanotechnology requires strong administrative systems that can explore the intricacies of this quickly propelling field.

The one of a kind properties of materials at the nanoscale, where aspects are normally somewhere in the range of 1 and 100 nanometers, present novel qualities that can contrast essentially from those at the large scale. These properties, for example, expanded surface region and adjusted substance reactivity, open up additional opportunities for making materials with improved functionalities. Nanotechnology has proactively tracked down applications in medication, where nanoparticles can be intended to target explicit cells for drug conveyance, and in gadgets, where nanoscale parts add to the improvement of more modest and more effective gadgets.

As the abilities of nanotechnology keep on growing, concerns have emerged with respect to its potential ecological, wellbeing, and security (EHS) gambles. The very ascribes that make nanoparticles important in different applications additionally bring up issues about their conduct in organic frameworks and the climate. In light of these worries, worldwide endeavors to manage nanotechnology have arisen, expecting to figure out some kind of harmony between encouraging advancement and guaranteeing the dependable turn of events and utilization of nanomaterials.

One noticeable discussion for global participation on nanotechnology guideline is the Association for Monetary Collaboration and Improvement (OECD). The OECD assumes a pivotal part in working with conversations among part nations to foster normal ways to deal with administrative difficulties. The Functioning Party on Fabricated Nanomaterials (WPMN), laid out in 2006, is at the front of these endeavors, zeroing in on the security of nanomaterials and advancing worldwide coordinated effort on testing and appraisal philosophies.

The WPMN's work incorporates a scope of exercises, including the improvement of test rules, the trading of data on risk evaluation and chance administration rehearses, and the distinguishing proof of regions where further examination is required. By encouraging cooperation among part nations, the OECD plans to upgrade the consistency and viability of administrative ways to deal with nanotechnology, perceiving that an orchestrated structure is fundamental in a globalized reality where nanomaterials and items can undoubtedly cross lines.

One of the difficulties in managing nanotechnology lies in the variety of uses and the comparing cluster of possible dangers. Nanomaterials can be designed for explicit purposes, and their properties can shift generally. Subsequently, a one-size-fits-all administrative methodology may not be reasonable. The OECD's endeavors center around creating versatile structures that can be applied to various areas while tending to the particular qualities of nanomaterials.

At the European level, the European Commission has been effectively engaged with fostering an extensive administrative structure for nanotechnology. The Enlistment, Assessment, Approval, and Limitation of Synthetic substances (REACH) guideline, a foundation of European synthetic compounds guideline, likewise applies to nanomaterials. REACH expects organizations to enlist and give data on the properties and utilizations of synthetic substances, including nanomaterials, to guarantee their protected use.

Notwithstanding Come to, the European Association (EU) has started explicit measures to address the extraordinary difficulties presented by nanotechnology. The EU's Nanomaterials Observatory fills in as a stage for gathering and dispersing data on nanomaterials, cultivating straightforwardness and mindfulness. Besides, the EU's Beauty care products Guideline incorporates arrangements for the marking and security appraisal of restorative items containing nanomaterials, perceiving the requirement for particular guidelines in unambiguous areas.

The administrative scene in the US has seen a comparative development in light of the developing conspicuousness of nanotechnology. The U.S. Ecological Security Office (EPA), the U.S. Food and Medication Organization (FDA), and the Word related Security and Wellbeing Organization (OSHA) have all been engaged with endeavors to comprehend and manage the natural, wellbeing, and security parts of nanomaterials.

The Public Nanotechnology Drive (NNI), sent off in 2000, fills in as the focal coordination point for nanotechnology innovative work across U.S. government organizations. While the NNI principally centers around progressing logical comprehension and advancing advancement, it additionally perceives the significance of tending to EHS concerns. The NNI's EHS Exploration Methodology tries to distinguish and focus on research requirements to guarantee the dependable improvement of nanotechnology.

In spite of these public and local endeavors, the worldwide idea of nanotechnology requires global coordinated effort to address administrative holes and guarantee a steady methodology. The Global Association for Normalization (ISO) has fostered a progression of guidelines connected with nanotechnology, covering wording, estimation techniques, and the evaluation of potential ecological and human wellbeing influences.

ISO Specialized Council 229 (ISO/TC 229) is devoted to normalizing nanotechnology and assumes an essential part in cultivating global collaboration. The advisory group unites specialists from around the world to foster agreement based norms that add to the protected and capable progression of nanotechnology. These guidelines cover a large number of subjects, including classification, metrology, and the portrayal of nanomaterials.

In the domain of word related wellbeing and security, the World Wellbeing Association (WHO) and the Global Work Association (ILO) have teamed up on rules for the protected treatment of nanomaterials in the work environment. The rules expect to safeguard laborers from potential perils related with nanomaterials and give proposals to gamble with appraisal and hazard the executives.

While these worldwide endeavors address huge steps in the guideline of nanotechnology, challenges continue. One such test is the powerful idea of nanotechnology itself. As the field keeps on developing, administrative systems should adjust to integrate new information and address arising chances. The speed of mechanical progression frequently exceeds the capacity of administrative bodies to create and carry out exhaustive rules.

One more test lies in the requirement for normalized strategies for surveying the dangers related with nanomaterials. Fluctuation in testing conventions and the absence of generally acknowledged philosophies frustrate the improvement of reliable administrative norms.

Endeavors to blend testing and evaluation techniques on a global scale, as exemplified by the OECD's work, mean to address this test and give an establishment to sound administrative direction.

Whether or not existing guidelines are adequate to address the interesting qualities of nanotechnology or on the other hand on the off chance that specific guidelines are required remaining parts a subject of discussion. Some contend that current systems, like Arrive at in Europe, can enough cover nanomaterials, while others fight that the particular properties of nanomaterials warrant committed guidelines. Finding some kind of harmony requires continuous cooperation among partners, including researchers, controllers, industry delegates, and common society.

Public commitment is a basic part of dependable nanotechnology administration. Informed public talk upgrades straightforwardness as well as guarantees that different points of view and concerns are viewed as in the administrative cycle. Public view of nanotechnology, affected by variables like media inclusion and cultural qualities, can essentially influence the acknowledgment and reception of nanoproducts.

The prudent guideline, which supporters making a preventive move notwithstanding vulnerability, has been conjured in conversations about nanotechnology guideline. Given the vulnerabilities encompassing the likely long haul effects of nanomaterials, defenders of the prudent rule contend for a mindful and proactive way to deal with guideline. Nonetheless, rivals fight that exorbitant safeguard could smother advancement and obstruct the acknowledgment of the cultural advantages of nanotechnology.

Moral contemplations likewise assume a focal part in conversations about nanotechnology guideline. The capacity to design materials at the nanoscale brings up moral issues about the expected abuse of such abilities. The double use nature of numerous innovations, where applications can have both valuable and destructive outcomes, adds a layer of intricacy to administrative independent direction. Finding some kind of harmony between advancing advancement and forestalling abuse requires cautious moral reflection and thought of more extensive cultural qualities.

Global joint effort on nanotechnology guideline is additionally confounded by international contemplations and varieties in administrative methods of reasoning among various nations. Spanning these holes requires discretionary endeavors, the sharing of best practices, and the acknowledgment that a blended methodology is in the aggregate interest of the worldwide local area. Drives like the Worldwide Harmonization of Hazard Appraisal in Nanotechnology (GloHRA), which looks to adjust risk evaluation rehearses around the world, address ventures toward accomplishing more prominent global combination.

7.2 The challenges of regulating a rapidly evolving field

In the complicated dance between mechanical development and administrative oversight, the difficulties of directing a quickly advancing field come to the very front. As the speed of logical and mechanical headways speeds up, controllers end up exploring an unfamiliar area, endeavoring to find some kind of harmony between cultivating development and protecting public government assistance. This challenge is especially articulated in fields like computerized reasoning, biotechnology, and nanotechnology, where the scene is continually moving, and the ramifications for society are significant.

One of the key difficulties of controlling quickly developing fields lies in the intrinsic pressure between the requirement for guideline and the basic of encouraging advancement. In the domain of man-made brainpower (man-made intelligence), for instance, the extraordinary potential is colossal, going from improved clinical diagnostics to independent vehicles. In any case, this potential is joined by moral worries, inquiries of responsibility, and fears of unseen side-effects. Controllers face the overwhelming assignment of creating systems that support the improvement of computer based intelligence while guaranteeing capable and moral use.

The actual idea of fast mechanical advancement presents challenges for controllers familiar with additional static scenes. Customary administrative models, frequently established in businesses with deep rooted standards, battle to adjust to the dynamism of arising fields. This versatility challenge is especially intense in areas where the speed of progress surpasses the limit of administrative bodies to keep up. In biotechnology, for example, quality altering methods like CRISPR-Cas9 have changed hereditary control, giving controllers moral and wellbeing contemplations that were impossible only a couple of years prior.

A huge obstacle in controlling quickly developing fields is the purported "pace hole" between mechanical headways and administrative reaction. As leap forwards happen at an uncommon speed, the time expected to draft, carry out, and uphold guidelines frequently falls behind. This delay can make an administrative void, passing on enterprises to work in an ill defined situation where standards and guidelines are as yet being formed. In fields like blockchain and digital currencies, where advancements like decentralized finance (DeFi) quickly reshape the monetary scene, controllers battle to stay up with the steadily developing scene.

In addition, the global aspect confuses administrative endeavors. Advances, especially those brought into the world in the computerized domain, rise above geological boundaries easily. An administrative structure that neglects to consider the worldwide idea of innovative progressions gambles becoming old. Coordination among countries becomes fundamental to guarantee a blended methodology and forestall administrative exchange, where substances could migrate to wards with less rigid guidelines.

In the domain of biotechnology, where quality altering and manufactured science hold the commitment of progressive clinical medicines, global coordinated effort becomes fundamental. The test lies in orchestrating administrative guidelines as well as in tending to different social and moral points of view on issues, for example, human germline altering. The moral contemplations encompassing biotechnological headways require a worldwide exchange to lay out shared belief and keep moral exceptions from taking advantage of administrative variations.

Another test emerges from the interdisciplinary idea of many quickly advancing fields. Advances like artificial intelligence and biotechnology don't fit perfectly into conventional administrative storehouses. All things being equal, they converge with different spaces, requiring an all encompassing and cooperative methodology from administrative bodies. In the field of independent vehicles, for example, guideline reaches out past transportation to envelop issues of information protection, network safety, and metropolitan preparation. Administrative systems should be adequately coordinated to include these diverse contemplations.

Moral contemplations add one more layer of intricacy to the administrative difficulties of quickly advancing fields. As innovations push the limits of what was once viewed as sci-fi, controllers should wrestle with the moral ramifications of their choices. In computer based intelligence, for instance, the utilization of AI calculations in recruiting processes brings up issues about predisposition and decency. Controllers are entrusted with creating structures that guarantee consistence with the law as well as maintain moral guidelines, reflecting cultural qualities.

The very attributes that gain arising advances useful assets for headway likewise render them vulnerable to abuse. This double use predicament is apparent in fields like manufactured science, where similar procedures utilized for creating life-saving treatments might actually be utilized for malevolent purposes. Making guidelines that moderate dangers without smothering helpful development requires a nuanced comprehension of the innovations at play and expectant measures to address possible abuse.

Besides, the democratization of innovation presents new difficulties. The availability of useful assets and information once restricted to specialists enables people and little gatherings to participate in mechanical exercises with worldwide ramifications. This shift brings up issues about how to direct and screen a scene where development can rise up out of surprising quarters. Digital currencies and blockchain, for example, challenge conventional ideas of monetary guideline as decentralized networks empower distributed exchanges outside the domain of customary monetary organizations.

The advancement of innovation likewise obscures the lines among shopper and maker, entangling the conventional administrative differentiation. In fields like 3D printing, people can make items at home, testing laid out administrative systems that expect an unmistakable depiction among producers and buyers.

The decentralized idea of specific advances moves controllers to reexamine their methodology, taking into account how to guarantee security and consistence in a scene where customary orders are dissolving.

In addition, the test of managing quickly advancing fields reaches out past innovation itself to the going with cultural movements. The ascent of the gig economy, worked with by computerized stages, challenges work guidelines intended for more customary manager representative connections. Controllers should wrestle with issues of laborers' privileges, professional stability, and social wellbeing nets in a scene where the actual idea of work is going through significant change.

Notwithstanding these difficulties, administrative sandboxes have arisen as exploratory spaces where new advances and plans of action can be tried in a controlled climate. These sandboxes give a center ground, considering development without compromising administrative oversight. They act as cauldrons for refining guidelines, empowering policymakers to notice this present reality ramifications of their choices before far reaching execution.

Public commitment turns into an imperative part of the administrative cycle in quickly developing fields. As advancements mold society in phenomenal ways, the consideration of different viewpoints guarantees that guidelines are compelling as well as intelligent of cultural qualities. Teaching general society about the ramifications of arising advances encourages an educated populace that can effectively partake in forming the administrative scene.

Notwithstanding these difficulties, there are examples where administrative structures have effectively adjusted to the fast speed of mechanical development. The field of drugs, for instance, has seen administrative components develop to oblige leap forwards in biotechnology and customized medication. Administrative organizations have executed assisted endorsement processes for inventive treatments while keeping up with thorough guidelines for wellbeing and viability.

In the domain of fintech, administrative bodies have participated in proactive discourse with industry partners to comprehend and address the difficulties acted by advancements such like blockchain and digital currencies. The Monetary Steadiness Oversight Committee (FSOC) in the US, for example, consistently surveys potential dangers related with arising monetary advancements and draws in with industry delegates to encourage a cooperative way to deal with guideline.

Global joint effort, as exemplified by associations like the Monetary Dependability Board (FSB) and the Worldwide Association of Protections Commissions (IOSCO), plays had an essential impact in creating normal guidelines for fintech guideline. This cooperative methodology perceives the worldwide idea of monetary frameworks and means to forestall administrative fracture that could hinder the development of imaginative monetary advances.

In the domain of room investigation, where privately owned businesses are progressively starting to lead the pack, administrative bodies have adjusted to the evolving scene. The Government Flight Organization (FAA) in the US, for example, has laid out an administrative system for business space exercises. This structure finds some kind of harmony between cultivating the prospering space industry and guaranteeing wellbeing and natural assurance.

The difficulties of managing a quickly developing field highlight the requirement for a proactive and versatile administrative methodology. Policymakers and controllers should develop a profound comprehension of arising advances, participate in continuous exchange with industry partners, and expect possible dangers and moral contemplations. The improvement of interdisciplinary skill inside administrative bodies becomes vital to address the multi-layered nature of quickly advancing fields.

7.3 The ethical and legal framework for nanotechnology research

Nanotechnology, working at the sub-atomic and nuclear scale, has opened new outskirts of logical investigation with extraordinary possible in different fields. As the abilities of nanotechnology progress, so do the moral and legitimate contemplations encompassing its exploration and applications. The crossing point of state of the art logical investigation and cultural ramifications requires a powerful moral and lawful system to direct the mindful turn of events and utilization of nanotechnology.

At the center of the moral contemplations in nanotechnology research lies the standard of capable development. Nanotechnology, with its capability to reform businesses from medication to energy, brings up issues about the cultural, ecological, and human wellbeing effects of its applications. Scientists, policymakers, and industry pioneers wrestle with the obligation to expect and moderate possible dangers while encouraging advancement to improve society.

One critical moral thought in nanotechnology spins around the potential ecological and wellbeing effects of nanomaterials. The extraordinary properties of materials at the nanoscale present vulnerabilities about their conduct in organic frameworks and biological systems. As nanoparticles track down applications in medication, hardware, and buyer items, questions emerge about their drawn out consequences for human wellbeing and the climate. Moral exploration rehearses request an exhaustive assessment of these expected dangers and a pledge to straightforwardness in revealing discoveries.

The moral system for nanotechnology research additionally includes the standards of equity and value. As nanotechnological headways unfurl, there is a gamble of compounding existing cultural imbalances. Admittance to the advantages of nanotechnology, whether in medical services or different areas, ought to be evenhanded, and endeavors ought to be made to forestall the formation of new variations. Analysts should be aware of the more extensive cultural ramifications of their work, taking a stab at inclusivity and guaranteeing that the advantages of nanotechnology are open to different populaces.

Moreover, the moral utilization of nanotechnology reaches out to issues of protection and security. The joining of nanoscale sensors and gadgets into ordinary items raises worries about the potential for intrusive observation. Moral rules should address the mindful utilization of nanotechnology to safeguard individual security and guarantee that its applications line up with cultural qualities. Finding some kind of harmony among development and moral contemplations is pivotal to building public trust and acknowledgment of nanotechnological headways.

Legitimate systems assume a corresponding part in molding the scene of nanotechnology research. Guidelines and regulations are fundamental to give an organized and responsible climate for specialists and industry players. Nonetheless, the powerful idea of nanotechnology presents difficulties for controllers, requiring a versatile lawful system that can stay up with innovative progressions.

One principal legitimate thought in nanotechnology research is the definition and order of nanomaterials. Laying out clear definitions is essential for administrative purposes, as it figures out which materials fall under unambiguous guidelines and norms. The meaning of nanomaterials frequently includes boundaries like size, surface region, and explicit properties, mirroring the special qualities of materials at the nanoscale.

In the European Association, for instance, the meaning of nanomaterials is necessary to the execution of the Enrollment, Assessment, Approval, and Limitation of Synthetic compounds (REACH) guideline. The definition took on by the EU considers the number dispersion by molecule size and explicit surface region, giving a premise to administrative prerequisites for nanomaterials in different areas.

The administrative scene for nanotechnology research shifts universally, with various nations taking on unmistakable methodologies. The US, through organizations like the Natural Assurance Organization (EPA) and the Food and Medication Organization (FDA), has been effectively participated in tending to the ecological and wellbeing effects of nanomaterials. The Public Nanotechnology Drive (NNI) fills in as an organizing stage for government nanotechnology research and administrative endeavors.

Conversely, the administrative methodology in Europe, drove by the European Commission, stresses a preparatory rule. The EU's Arrive at guideline, as well as unambiguous guidelines for areas like beauty care products and food, integrates contemplations for nanomaterials. The European Synthetics Organization (ECHA) assumes a critical part in executing and directing the administrative structure for nanomaterials under REACH.

Global associations likewise add to the advancement of lawful systems for nanotechnology research. The Association for Monetary Participation and Advancement (OECD) has been effectively participated in blending ways to deal with the guideline of nanomaterials.

The OECD's Functioning Party on Produced Nanomaterials (WPMN) centers around issues of wellbeing and hazard evaluation, working with global collaboration and data trade.

Notwithstanding, the adequacy of lawful systems relies upon their capacity to adjust to the fast speed of mechanical headway. Nanotechnology's interdisciplinary nature challenges conventional administrative storehouses, requiring an organized and adaptable methodology. Lawful structures should be expectant, equipped for tending to possible dangers before they become inescapable, while trying not to smother advancement with excessively troublesome guidelines.

The licensed innovation (IP) scene further muddles the legitimate system for nanotechnology research. As scientists and organizations make leap forwards in nano-technology, issues of protecting, permitting, and innovation move become central. Adjusting the need to boost advancement through IP security with the basic of guaranteeing inescapable admittance to new innovations is a continuous test.

Patent workplaces overall wrestle with the exceptional intricacies of nanotechnology licenses. Deciding the oddity and creativity of nanotechnological developments requires a nuanced comprehension of the logical standards at play. The lawful structure should find some kind of harmony between giving creators the motivating forces to put resources into nanotechnology research and forestalling the restraining infrastructure of fundamental advances that could impede further development.

Worldwide cooperation becomes fundamental in tending to the worldwide diffi-culties presented by the legitimate and moral elements of nanotechnology research. Fitting legitimate structures, sharing prescribed procedures, and organizing adminis-trative endeavors add to a more durable and viable methodology. Associations like the Global Association for Normalization (ISO) pursue normalizing phrasing, estimation strategies, and wellbeing rules for nanotechnology on a worldwide scale.

Moral rules and legitimate systems should likewise address the potential double use nature of nanotechnology research. The very innovative progressions that hold guarantee for further developing medical care or tending to ecological difficulties could be reused for malevolent purposes. The moral obligation stretches out to expecting and moderating the dangers of abuse while encouraging the positive uses of nanotechnology.

Public commitment arises as a pivotal part of both moral and lawful contempla-tions in nanotechnology research. The intricacies of nanotechnology make it basic to include the general population in dynamic cycles. As nanotechnological progressions can possibly affect day to day existence, public mindfulness, understanding, and acknowledgment are indispensable for the capable turn of events and use of nano-technology.

Schooling and correspondence endeavors ought to overcome any barrier between researchers, policymakers, and people in general. Moral contemplations ought to be coordinated into logical instruction, encouraging a culture of dependable direct among scientists. Public exchange gatherings, informed by moral standards, can give a stage to examining the cultural ramifications of nanotechnology and integrating different points of view into dynamic cycles.

Moreover, straightforwardness in research rehearses is fundamental to building public trust. Open correspondence about the objectives, techniques, and possible dangers of nanotechnology research adds to informed public talk. Scientists and foundations should be proactive in sharing data, tending to worries, and including general society in molding the moral and lawful structures that administer nano-technology.

The moral and legitimate system for nanotechnology research additionally stretches out to contemplations of worldwide administration. Nanotechnology, by its temperament, rises above public lines, and worldwide cooperation is vital for address the difficulties it presents extensively. Peaceful accords, shows, and coordinated efforts ought to reflect shared values and standards, guaranteeing that the advantages and dangers of nanotechnology are overseen aggregately.

As nanotechnology keeps on advancing, the moral and legitimate structure should develop couple. The versatile idea of these systems, equipped for answering arising difficulties and open doors, is fundamental for exploring the complicated landscape of nanotechnology research. A blended and expectant methodology, grounded in moral standards, lawful guidelines, and worldwide collaboration, will add to the mindful and valuable improvement of nanotechnology to improve society.

Chapter 8

Scientists, Ethicists, and Policymakers

Nanotechnology, working at the sub-atomic and nuclear scale, has opened new boondocks of logical investigation with groundbreaking likely in different fields. As the capacities of nanotechnology progress, so do the moral and legitimate contemplations encompassing its examination and applications. The crossing point of state of the art logical investigation and cultural ramifications requires a powerful moral and lawful structure to direct the dependable turn of events and utilization of nanotechnology.

At the center of the moral contemplations in nanotechnology research lies the standard of dependable advancement. Nanotechnology, with its capability to alter ventures from medication to energy, brings up issues about the cultural, ecological, and human wellbeing effects of its applications. Scientists, policymakers, and industry pioneers wrestle with the obligation to expect and moderate likely dangers while encouraging advancement to improve society.

One vital moral thought in nanotechnology rotates around the potential ecological and wellbeing effects of nanomaterials. The novel properties of materials at the nanoscale present vulnerabilities about their conduct in natural frameworks and biological systems. As nanoparticles track down applications in medication, gadgets, and buyer items, questions emerge about their drawn out impacts on human wellbeing and the climate. Moral exploration rehearses request an exhaustive assessment of these likely dangers and a guarantee to straightforwardness in revealing discoveries.

The moral structure for nanotechnology research additionally envelops the standards of equity and value. As nanotechnological progressions unfurl, there is a gamble of compounding existing cultural imbalances. Admittance to the advantages of nanotechnology, whether in medical care or different areas, ought to be evenhanded, and endeavors ought to be made to forestall the production of new variations. Analysts should be perceptive of the more extensive cultural ramifications of their work, taking a stab at inclusivity and guaranteeing that the advantages of nanotechnology are open to different populaces.

Moreover, the moral utilization of nanotechnology reaches out to issues of protection and security. The joining of nanoscale sensors and gadgets into ordinary articles raises worries about the potential for obtrusive observation. Moral rules should address the dependable utilization of nanotechnology to safeguard individual protection and guarantee that its applications line up with cultural qualities.

Finding some kind of harmony among development and moral contemplations is critical to building public trust and acknowledgment of nanotechnological headways.

Legitimate structures assume a correlative part in molding the scene of nanotechnology research. Guidelines and regulations are fundamental to give an organized and responsible climate for scientists and industry players. Nonetheless, the unique idea of nanotechnology presents difficulties for controllers, requiring a versatile legitimate system that can stay up with innovative progressions.

One crucial lawful thought in nanotechnology research is the definition and grouping of nanomaterials. Laying out clear definitions is critical for administrative purposes, as it figures out which materials fall under unambiguous guidelines and principles. The meaning of nanomaterials frequently includes boundaries like size, surface region, and explicit properties, mirroring the special qualities of materials at the nanoscale.

In the European Association, for instance, the meaning of nanomaterials is basic to the execution of the Enlistment, Assessment, Approval, and Limitation of Synthetic substances (REACH) guideline. The definition embraced by the EU considers the number circulation by molecule size and explicit surface region, giving a premise to administrative necessities for nanomaterials in different areas.

The administrative scene for nanotechnology research changes internationally, with various nations embracing particular methodologies. The US, through organizations like the Natural Security Office (EPA) and the Food and Medication Organization (FDA), has been effectively participated in tending to the ecological and wellbeing effects of nanomaterials. The Public Nanotechnology Drive (NNI) fills in as an organizing stage for government nanotechnology research and administrative endeavors.

Conversely, the administrative methodology in Europe, drove by the European Commission, underscores a preparatory rule. The EU's Arrive at guideline, as well as unambiguous guidelines for areas like beauty care products and food, consolidates contemplations for nanomaterials. The European Synthetics Office (ECHA) assumes a critical part in carrying out and supervising the administrative system for nanomaterials under REACH.

Global associations additionally add to the improvement of lawful structures for nanotechnology research. The Association for Financial Participation and Improvement (OECD) has been effectively participated in blending ways to deal with the guideline of nanomaterials. The OECD's Functioning Party on Fabricated Nanomaterials (WPMN) centers around issues of security and chance appraisal, working with worldwide participation and data trade.

In any case, the adequacy of legitimate systems relies upon their capacity to adjust to the fast speed of mechanical headway. Nanotechnology's interdisciplinary nature challenges conventional administrative storehouses, requiring a planned and adaptable methodology. Legitimate systems should be expectant, equipped for tending to possible dangers before they become far and wide, while trying not to smother development with excessively difficult guidelines.

The protected innovation (IP) scene further convolutes the lawful structure for nanotechnology research. As scientists and organizations make leap forwards in nanotechnology, issues of protecting, permitting, and innovation move become central. Adjusting the need to boost development through IP assurance with the basic of guaranteeing inescapable admittance to new advancements is a continuous test.

Patent workplaces overall wrestle with the interesting intricacies of nanotechnology licenses. Deciding the oddity and imagination of nanotechnological developments requires a nuanced comprehension of the logical standards at play. The legitimate structure should find some kind of harmony between furnishing designers with the motivating forces to put resources into nanotechnology research and forestalling the restraining infrastructure of fundamental advancements that could obstruct further development.

Worldwide coordinated effort becomes fundamental in tending to the worldwide difficulties presented by the legitimate and moral components of nanotechnology research. Orchestrating legitimate structures, sharing prescribed procedures, and organizing administrative endeavors add to a more firm and compelling methodology. Associations like the Worldwide Association for Normalization (ISO) pursue normalizing wording, estimation techniques, and wellbeing rules for nanotechnology on a global scale.

Moral rules and lawful structures should likewise address the potential double use nature of nanotechnology research. The very innovative headways that hold guarantee for further developing medical services or tending to natural difficulties could be reused for noxious purposes. The moral obligation stretches out to expecting and relieving the dangers of abuse while encouraging the positive uses of nanotechnology.

Public commitment arises as a critical part of both moral and lawful contemplations in nanotechnology research. The intricacies of nanotechnology make it basic to include general society in dynamic cycles. As nanotechnological progressions can possibly affect day to day existence, public mindfulness, understanding, and acknowledgment are fundamental for the capable turn of events and use of nanotechnology.

Schooling and correspondence endeavors ought to overcome any barrier between researchers, policymakers, and people in general. Moral contemplations ought to be coordinated into logical schooling, cultivating a culture of dependable lead among specialists.

Public discourse gatherings, informed by moral standards, can give a stage to examining the cultural ramifications of nanotechnology and integrating different viewpoints into dynamic cycles.

Besides, straightforwardness in research rehearses is essential to building public trust. Open correspondence about the objectives, strategies, and likely dangers of nanotechnology research adds to informed public talk. Specialists and organizations should be proactive in sharing data, tending to worries, and including people in general in molding the moral and legitimate structures that administer nanotechnology.

The moral and lawful system for nanotechnology research likewise stretches out to contemplations of worldwide administration. Nanotechnology, by its inclination, rises above public lines, and global joint effort is fundamental for address the difficulties it presents extensively. Peaceful accords, shows, and joint efforts ought to reflect shared values and standards, guaranteeing that the advantages and dangers of nanotechnology are overseen all in all.

As nanotechnology keeps on advancing, the moral and lawful system should develop couple. The versatile idea of these structures, equipped for answering arising difficulties and amazing open doors, is fundamental for exploring the intricate landscape of nanotechnology research. An orchestrated and expectant methodology, grounded in moral standards, legitimate guidelines, and worldwide collaboration, will add to the dependable and gainful improvement of nanotechnology to improve society.

8.1 Perspectives from leading experts in the field

Researchers, ethicists, and policymakers structure a ternion of key partners in the unique exchange between logical advancement, moral contemplations, and the improvement of strategies that shape the cultural effect of arising innovations. This joint effort is especially critical in fields like computerized reasoning (man-made intelligence), biotechnology, and nanotechnology, where the potential advantages are immense, however moral worries and administrative difficulties flourish.

Researchers, as designers of development, bear the obligation of pushing the limits of information and mechanical capacities. In the domain of man-made intelligence, scientists are creating calculations that can independently learn and decide, a field known as AI. The moral contemplations encompassing artificial intelligence include inquiries of predisposition in calculations, straightforwardness in dynamic cycles, and the expected effect on business and protection.

Ethicists, then again, contribute a basic point of view that rises above the specialized domain. Their job is to examine the ramifications of logical headways from the perspective of virtues, cultural standards, and basic liberties.

In computer based intelligence, ethicists might raise worries about the moral utilization of facial acknowledgment innovation, the potential for algorithmic segregation, and the responsibility of independent frameworks. They assume a crucial part in guaranteeing that logical advancement lines up with more extensive moral standards.

Policymakers, sitting at the crossing point of science and morals, face the difficult errand of creating guidelines and rules that offset advancement with cultural prosperity. With regards to man-made intelligence, policymakers should explore issues like information security, algorithmic responsibility, and the moral utilization of computer based intelligence in regions like law enforcement and medical services. Making powerful arrangements requires a comprehension of both the logical complexities and the moral ramifications of arising advances.

In the area of biotechnology, researchers are opening the capability of quality altering advancements like CRISPR-Cas9, offering uncommon capacities to control the hereditary code. Ethicists assume a crucial part in directing the dependable utilization of these innovations, taking into account the moral ramifications of human germline altering, the potential for fashioner children, and the ethical inquiries encompassing quality altering in horticulture.

Policymakers, confronted with the fast headways in biotechnology, wrestle with the need to direct quality altering to forestall abuse while encouraging advancements with the possibility to fix hereditary illnesses. The moral and legitimate contemplations in biotechnology reach out to issues like the responsibility for data, the guideline of hereditarily adjusted organic entities (GMOs), and the ramifications of hereditary information in protection and business.

In nanotechnology, researchers dive into the control of materials at the nuclear and sub-atomic scale, prompting advancements with applications in medication, gadgets, and materials science. Ethicists examine the potential natural and wellbeing effects of nanomaterials, the evenhanded dispersion of advantages, and the moral utilization of nanotechnology in reconnaissance and protection.

Policymakers, working at the nexus of logical headways and moral contemplations in nanotechnology, wrestle with the test of making guidelines that guarantee the protected and mindful advancement of nanomaterials. The legitimate systems for nanotechnology should resolve issues, for example, the definition and arrangement of nanomaterials, wellbeing guidelines, and the insurance of laborers and the climate.

The cooperation between researchers, ethicists, and policymakers is definitely not a direct cycle yet an iterative and dynamic discourse. Researchers push the limits of what is potential, ethicists basically analyze the ramifications, and policymakers make an interpretation of these contemplations into guidelines that guide the moral turn of events and utilization of innovations. This cooperative interaction is fundamental for exploring the intricacies of the 21st-century innovative scene.

In the space of artificial intelligence, the cooperation between researchers, ethicists, and policymakers is exemplified by progressing endeavors to address the moral difficulties related with AI. Researchers are creating calculations that gain from tremendous datasets, raising worries about algorithmic predisposition and reasonableness. Ethicists contribute by examining the ramifications of one-sided calculations, upholding for straightforwardness in artificial intelligence navigation, and underscoring the significance of human oversight in basic areas.

Policymakers, perceiving the moral components of man-made intelligence, are participated in the advancement of guidelines that advance decency, responsibility, and straightforwardness. Drives like the European Association's Overall Information Insurance Guideline (GDPR) incorporate arrangements connected with mechanized independent direction, expecting to guarantee that people are not expose to prejudicial practices. Policymakers team up with ethicists to make an interpretation of moral standards into significant guidelines that oversee the turn of events and organization of simulated intelligence innovations.

Moral contemplations in computer based intelligence reach out to issues of security, as calculations examine tremendous measures of individual information to settle on forecasts and choices. Researchers chipping away at simulated intelligence applications should wrestle with the compromise between the advantages of customized administrations and the expected encroachment on individual security. Ethicists contribute by supporting for security safeguarding advancements, informed assent, and hearty information assurance guidelines.

Policymakers assume a urgent part in laying out lawful systems that safeguard individual protection in the period of computer based intelligence. The improvement of guidelines, for example, the California Buyer Security Act (CCPA) in the US and the GDPR in the European Association, mirrors an acknowledgment of the moral significance of protection in the computerized time. Policymakers team up with researchers and ethicists to find some kind of harmony among development and the security of individual freedoms in the advancing scene of computer based intelligence.

In addition, the cooperative endeavors between researchers, ethicists, and policymakers in artificial intelligence reach out to inquiries of straightforwardness and responsibility. As man-made intelligence frameworks become progressively complicated, the "discovery" nature of certain calculations raises worries about the absence of straightforwardness in dynamic cycles. Ethicists contribute by supporting for logical computer based intelligence and moral rules that focus on straightforwardness and responsibility.

Policymakers, answering moral contemplations, make progress toward laying out guidelines that require straightforwardness in man-made intelligence frameworks. Drives, for example, the Algorithmic Responsibility Act in the US expect to guarantee that computerized dynamic cycles are reasonable and responsible.

Policymakers draw in with researchers and ethicists to foster norms that balance the requirement for straightforwardness with the restrictive worries of innovation engineers.

In biotechnology, the coordinated effort between researchers, ethicists, and policymakers is obvious in the continuous talk encompassing quality altering advancements. Researchers, driven by the possibility to fix hereditary illnesses and improve human capacities, are at the very front of growing incredible assets like CRISPR-Cas9. Ethicists contribute by inspecting the ethical ramifications of quality altering, taking into account inquiries of assent, value, and the change of the human germline.

Policymakers, perceiving the moral intricacies of quality altering, are participated in the improvement of guidelines that oversee its utilization. The worldwide discussion encompassing the moral contemplations of human germline altering, exemplified by occasions like the Global Highest point on Human Quality Altering, mirrors the cooperative endeavors of researchers, ethicists, and policymakers to lay out a structure that guides mindful examination and applications.

Moral contemplations in biotechnology stretch out past human quality altering to issues like hereditarily adjusted organic entities (GMOs) in agribusiness. Researchers dealing with hereditarily altered crops should explore inquiries of ecological effect, food handling, and the evenhanded dispersion of advantages. Ethicists contribute by looking at the moral components of changing the hereditary cosmetics of organic entities in manners that influence environments and worldwide food frameworks.

Policymakers, perceiving the moral components of biotechnology, pursue laying out guidelines that guarantee the protected and capable utilization of hereditary advances. The Cartagena Convention on Biosafety, a worldwide deal, addresses the moral contemplations of GMOs by giving a structure to the protected exchange, dealing with, and utilization of living changed organic entities. Policymakers team up with researchers and ethicists to foster guidelines that balance the expected advantages of biotechnology with the moral goals of ecological and public wellbeing.

In nanotechnology, the cooperation between researchers, ethicists, and policymakers is exemplified by endeavors to address the potential ecological and wellbeing effects of nanomaterials. Researchers, driven by the commitment of creative applications in medication, hardware, and materials science, are at the cutting edge of nanotechnological research. Ethicists contribute by examining the moral ramifications of nanotechnology, taking into account inquiries of chance appraisal, impartial dissemination of advantages, and the moral utilization of nanomaterials in observation and protection.

Policymakers, perceiving the moral contemplations in nanotechnology, take part in the improvement of guidelines that guide its dependable turn of events and use. The coordinated effort between established researchers, ethicists, and policymakers is clear in drives like the Association for Monetary Participation and Advancement's (OECD) Working Party on Fabricated Nanomaterials (WPMN), which centers around security.

8.2 Debates and discussions on the future of nanotechnology

Nanotechnology, working at the size of particles and particles, has ignited broad discussions and conversations about its expected advantages, moral ramifications, and cultural effect. As researchers push the limits of what is conceivable at the nanoscale, a range of viewpoints arises, going from excited confidence to wary incredulity. The multi-layered nature of these discussions mirrors the intricacy of nanotechnology and its broad ramifications for assorted fields, including medication, gadgets, and materials science.

One focal discussion rotates around the possible advantages of nanotechnology in medication, especially in the domain of diagnostics and therapeutics. Defenders contend that nanotechnology holds the commitment of upsetting medical services by empowering designated drug conveyance, early illness discovery, and customized medication. Nanoscale particles and gadgets, when planned with accuracy, can explore the intricacies of the human body, conveying restorative specialists straightforwardly to sick cells while limiting secondary effects.

Nanomedicine, as this field is known, can possibly upgrade the viability of therapies for conditions going from malignant growth to neurodegenerative infections. Nano-particles can be designed to convey tranquilizes specifically to disease cells, diminishing the effect on solid tissues. Moreover, nanoscale imaging advancements offer exceptional experiences into cell and sub-atomic cycles, empowering early identification and intercession.

Nonetheless, this hopeful view is met with distrust and moral worries. Pundits bring up issues about the drawn out wellbeing of nanoscale clinical mediations and the possible potentially negative side-effects of controlling organic frameworks at such a crucial level. The obscure connections between designed nanoparticles and the human body lead to worries about poisonousness, insusceptible reactions, and unanticipated incidental effects that may just become clear after inescapable execution.

Also, the moral ramifications of nanomedicine stretch out to issues like availability and value. In the event that nanotechnology prompts weighty clinical medicines, questions emerge about who will approach these advancements. Will nanomedicine worsen existing medical care abberations, or could administrative structures and moral contemplations at any point guarantee that the advantages are disseminated evenhandedly? Discusses encompassing the morals of nanomedicine highlight the requirement for a cautious harmony among development and cultural prosperity.

In the domain of hardware, the capability of nanotechnology to upset figuring and data stockpiling has filled serious discussions. The quest for scaling down, driven by Moore's Regulation, has reached the nanoscale, with scientists investigating the advancement of nanoscale semiconductors and memory gadgets. Advocates contend that these headways will prompt quicker, more productive, and energy-saving electronic gadgets, making ready for the up and coming age of registering.

The coming of quantum figuring, a field that use the standards of quantum mechanics at the nanoscale, adds one more layer to the discussions on the fate of hardware. Quantum PCs can possibly tackle complex issues dramatically quicker than old style PCs, with applications in cryptography, improvement, and medication disclosure. Hopeful people imagine a change in perspective in processing capacities, while doubters raise worries about the specialized difficulties, security suggestions, and moral contemplations encompassing quantum figuring.

Pundits additionally question the ecological effect of the hardware business' constant quest for scaling down. The creation and removal of nanoscale electronic parts raise worries about asset consumption, electronic waste, and the arrival of possibly risky materials into the climate. Adjusting the expected advantages of nanoelectronics with the environmental impression of its turn of events and use turns into an essential issue of dispute in these discussions.

Materials science, with its emphasis on planning and controlling materials at the nanoscale, is at the bleeding edge of nanotechnology discusses. Nanomaterials show extraordinary properties that can improve the presentation of existing materials or make completely new materials with novel functionalities. The potential applications range from lightweight and solid nanocomposites to nanoscale sensors and coatings with customized properties.

Banters on nanomaterials frequently focus on inquiries of wellbeing, risk evaluation, and natural effect. As nanomaterials track down applications in purchaser items, from apparel to food bundling, concerns arise about the likely arrival of nanoparticles into the climate and their communications with living creatures. Scientists and controllers wrestle with the test of evaluating the dangers presented by nanomaterials, taking into account factors like poisonousness, perseverance, and bioaccumulation.

The moral contemplations encompassing nanomaterials stretch out to issues of straightforwardness and public mindfulness. Pundits contend that the utilization of nanomaterials in purchaser items might outperform how we might interpret their drawn out impacts, possibly uncovering both the climate and buyers to unexpected dangers. The moral obligation to impart straightforwardly about the utilization of nanomaterials, direct thorough security evaluations, and include the general population in dynamic cycles turns into a point of convergence in these discussions.

One of the overall discussions in nanotechnology rotates around the cultural ramifications of its broad reception. Defenders contend that nanotechnology can possibly address squeezing worldwide difficulties, from clean energy creation to water decontamination. Nanomaterials, with their interesting properties, can add to the advancement of maintainable innovations that moderate natural effect.

Cynics, notwithstanding, express worries about the potentially negative side-effects of conveying nanotechnology for a huge scope. The "dark goo" situation, a speculative circumstance where self-repeating nanobots go crazy, is much of the time refered to as an Armageddon situation in the discussions on nanotechnology. While such a situation stays speculative and faces critical specialized difficulties, it highlights the requirement for cautious thought of the likely dangers and moral components of conveying nanotechnology at a worldwide scale.

The democratization of nanotechnology, with the rising openness of devices and information, acquaints new aspects with the discussions. As people and little gatherings gain the capacity to participate in nanotechnological exercises, questions emerge about the requirement for administrative systems, oversight, and dependable direct.

The potential for double use applications, where nanotechnology could be reused for pernicious purposes, includes earnestness to conversations administration and security.

The crossing point of nanotechnology with fields like man-made brainpower, biotechnology, and data innovation adds layers of intricacy to the discussions. The union of these groundbreaking advancements, frequently alluded to as NBIC intermingling (nano-bio-data cogno combination), brings up issues about the cooperative energies, moral contemplations, and cultural effects of their consolidated turn of events.

The moral discussions encompassing NBIC assembly reach out to inquiries of human upgrade, mental expansion, and the obscuring of limits among man and machine. As progressions in nanotechnology empower exact control at the cell and brain levels, moral contemplations about the potential for improving human abilities and the ramifications for individual personality and independence come to the cutting edge.

The cooperative endeavors between researchers, ethicists, and policymakers are urgent for exploring the discussions on the fate of nanotechnology. Researchers, driven by the quest for information and mechanical development, should draw in with moral contemplations from the commencement of their exploration. Incorporating moral standards into the plan and advancement of nanotechnologies guarantees that likely dangers and cultural ramifications are tended to proactively.

Ethicists, by examining the moral components of nanotechnology, contribute a basic viewpoint that goes past specialized practicality. Their part in recognizing expected chances, evaluating the moral ramifications of various applications, and cultivating public discourse is fundamental for dependable advancement. Ethicists act as supporters for moral contemplations inside mainstream researchers, industry, and policymaking circles.

Policymakers, working at the crossing point of logical progressions and moral contemplations, face the test of making an interpretation of moral standards into significant guidelines. The advancement of lawful systems that guide the mindful turn of events and utilization of nanotechnologies requires a comprehension of both the logical complexities and the moral ramifications. Policymakers team up with researchers and ethicists to work out some kind of harmony among advancement and cultural prosperity.

The cooperative model between researchers, ethicists, and policymakers additionally reaches out to public commitment. Educated and connected with residents contribute different viewpoints to the discussions on the fate of nanotechnology. Public exchange gatherings, instructive drives, and participatory dynamic cycles guarantee that the cultural ramifications of nanotechnology are thought about aggregately.

In addition, worldwide coordinated effort becomes fundamental in tending to the worldwide difficulties presented by nanotechnology. As nanotechnological headways rise above public boundaries, blending moral contemplations, legitimate systems, and administrative methodologies on a global scale becomes fundamental. Associations like the Association for Monetary Collaboration and Improvement (OECD) assume a part in working with worldwide collaboration and data exchange.

8.3 The importance of interdisciplinary collaboration

In the quickly developing scene of logical and mechanical headways, the significance of interdisciplinary joint effort has become progressively obvious. Interdisciplinary coordinated effort alludes to the reconciliation of information, systems, and viewpoints from numerous disciplines to address complex difficulties and create inventive arrangements. This cooperative methodology recognizes the interconnectedness of different fields of study and perceives that some genuine issues can't be really handled inside the limits of a solitary discipline. The collaboration made by uniting assorted ability encourages inventiveness, speeds up critical thinking, and elevates comprehensive ways to deal with understanding and resolving multi-layered issues.

One vital part of interdisciplinary coordinated effort is the acknowledgment that perplexing difficulties frequently require experiences from different areas. Conventional disciplinary limits can be restricting while managing issues that length numerous aspects. For instance, tending to environmental change includes understanding the barometrical and land processes as well as thinking about financial variables, political elements, and social impacts.

By incorporating information from climatology, financial matters, political theory, and human sciences, interdisciplinary joint effort empowers a more thorough comprehension of the interconnected elements adding to environmental change and works with the improvement of powerful moderation and variation techniques.

In the domain of medical care, the significance of interdisciplinary coordinated effort is clear in the field of translational medication. Translational medication looks to overcome any barrier between essential logical exploration and the advancement of functional applications for patient consideration. Uniting scientists from different fields like sub-atomic science, clinical medication, designing, and information science considers a consistent progression of data and mastery. This cooperative exertion speeds up the interpretation of logical disclosures into clinical advancements, at last helping patients by further developing diagnostics, medicines, and in general medical services results.

Besides, interdisciplinary coordinated effort assumes a vital part in tending to the complicated difficulties presented by worldwide general wellbeing emergencies, as exemplified by the Coronavirus pandemic. Battling a pandemic requires mastery from different disciplines, including virology, the study of disease transmission, medication, general wellbeing, information science, sociologies, and that's just the beginning. The cooperative endeavors of researchers, medical care experts, policymakers, and social researchers have been fundamental in understanding the infection, creating immunizations, executing general wellbeing measures, and tending to the more extensive cultural effects of the pandemic.

The interdisciplinary methodology isn't restricted to the normal and clinical sciences; it is similarly fundamental in resolving complex social issues. For example, handling destitution requires experiences from financial aspects, social science, political theory, and metropolitan preparation. Understanding the complexities of destitution includes investigating monetary pointers as well as thinking about friendly designs, social elements, and authentic settings. Interdisciplinary coordinated effort in this setting considers a more nuanced and exhaustive way to deal with planning viable neediness mitigation procedures.

With regards to innovation and development, interdisciplinary coordinated effort is driving forward leaps in fields like man-made reasoning (man-made intelligence), nanotechnology, and materials science. Simulated intelligence, for instance, includes software engineering and designing as well as morals, brain science, and legitimate investigations. Guaranteeing that man-made intelligence frameworks are created and sent dependably requires interdisciplinary cooperation to resolve issues of inclination, straightforwardness, responsibility, and the moral ramifications of independent navigation.

Nanotechnology, working at the crossing point of physical science, science, science, and materials science, represents the intrinsically interdisciplinary nature of logical request. The control of materials at the nanoscale opens up additional opportunities in medication, hardware, energy, and materials plan.

Scientists from assorted disciplines team up to investigate the expected utilizations of nanotechnology, addressing difficulties connected with wellbeing, morals, and the cultural ramifications of this groundbreaking field.

In materials science, the plan of cutting edge materials with custom-made properties includes aptitude from science, physical science, designing, and computational demonstrating. Interdisciplinary coordinated effort in this field has prompted the improvement of materials with upgraded strength, conductivity, and other advantageous qualities. These materials track down applications in many businesses, from aviation to sustainable power, featuring the groundbreaking effect of cooperative endeavors across disciplines.

The significance of interdisciplinary coordinated effort isn't restricted to the logical and specialized areas; it reaches out to the humanities and sociologies. In figuring out complex social peculiarities, like relocation, imbalance, and social elements, interdisciplinary points of view improve the examination and deal a more thorough comprehension. For instance, concentrating on movement requires experiences from humanism, financial aspects, political theory, geology, and humanities to catch the different variables affecting transitory examples and their effect on social orders.

Instructive organizations assume a vital part in cultivating interdisciplinary joint effort by separating customary storehouses between scholarly disciplines. Interdisciplinary projects and research focuses give a stage to researchers and understudies to take part in cooperative undertakings that rise above disciplinary limits. These drives develop a culture of transparency, interest, and shared picking up, empowering people to investigate associations between various fields and add to the combination of information.

The advantages of interdisciplinary coordinated effort reach out past the domain of scholarly exploration. In the business and industry areas, associations progressively perceive the worth of interdisciplinary groups in driving development and tackling complex issues. Cross-practical groups that unite people with different abilities and skill are better prepared to address the multi-layered difficulties presented by a quickly changing worldwide scene. The capacity to explore the convergences between innovation, morals, financial matters, and social elements turns into an upper hand in this present reality where issues are seldom restricted to a solitary space.

Interdisciplinary coordinated effort is especially pertinent in tending to the perplexing and interconnected nature of ecological difficulties. Environmental change, biodiversity misfortune, and natural corruption require a comprehensive comprehension that goes past conventional disciplinary limits. Researchers, policymakers, business analysts, and sociologists should team up to foster practical arrangements that offset biological respectability with social and financial contemplations. The interdisciplinary methodology in natural science and strategy is vital for thinking up versatile and versatile procedures that address the main drivers of ecological difficulties.

Notwithstanding, the execution of interdisciplinary cooperation accompanies its own arrangement of difficulties. Conventional scholar and institutional designs frequently focus on disciplinary specialization, making it moving for scientists to take part in interdisciplinary work. Boundaries like contrasts in language, procedures, and research needs can hinder compelling joint effort between disciplines. In addition, the assessment and acknowledgment components in scholarly world, like residency and advancement standards, may not sufficiently esteem interdisciplinary commitments, deterring researchers from wandering past the limits of their disciplines.

Defeating these difficulties requires a change in scholastic culture and institutional help for interdisciplinary drives. Perceiving and remunerating cooperative and interdisciplinary exploration through refreshed advancement and residency rules can boost researchers to participate in such undertakings. Organizations can lay out interdisciplinary exploration communities, work with cross-disciplinary courses and studios, and give subsidizing valuable open doors explicitly intended to help cooperative undertakings.

Additionally, cultivating compelling interdisciplinary coordinated effort requires the advancement of correspondence and cooperation abilities. Scientists should be proficient at imparting their thoughts across disciplinary limits, deciphering complex ideas for an assorted crowd, and valuing the points of view and systems of teammates from various fields. Interdisciplinary preparation projects and studios can add to the improvement of these abilities, planning scientists for effective joint effort in interdisciplinary settings.

The significance of interdisciplinary joint effort is highlighted by the undeniably intricate and interconnected nature of worldwide difficulties. From general well-being emergencies to environmental change, no single discipline holds every one of the responses. Embracing an interdisciplinary methodology takes into consideration a more all encompassing comprehension of perplexing issues, empowers imaginative critical thinking, and adds to the improvement of manageable arrangements.

The capability of interdisciplinary cooperation is exemplified by drives that address the Assembled Countries Maintainable Improvement Objectives (SDGs). Accomplishing objectives like zero appetite, clean water and disinfection, and quality training requires joint effort between researchers, policymakers, experts, and networks. The SDGs act as a plan for interdisciplinary endeavors that unite different skill to make positive and enduring effects on a worldwide scale.

Chapter 9

A Call to Action

In the turbulent scene of contemporary society, where the reverberations of progress resonate through each feature of human life, a source of inspiration reverberates with a direness that can't be disregarded. The world stands at a cliff, wavering on the edge of phenomenal difficulties and potential open doors, requesting an aggregate reaction that rises above the limits of individual interests. A call entices humankind to transcend the chaos of disagreement, to join in reason and manufacture a way toward a future that is practical, impartial, and just.

At the core of this source of inspiration is the acknowledgment that the ongoing direction of our worldwide local area is unreasonable. The planet moans under the heaviness of ecological corruption, as environmental change, deforestation, and contamination compromise the sensitive equilibrium of biological systems. The outcomes of our activities are presently not far off ghosts however quick real factors, appearing in outrageous climate occasions, loss of biodiversity, and the removal of weak networks. The basic to address these natural difficulties isn't only a moral decision however an endurance need.

At the same time, the social texture of our reality is fraying at the creases. Imbalances endure, sustaining a pattern of destitution, segregation, and disappointment that sabotages the actual standards of equity and equity. The gap between the advantaged and the underestimated broadens, cultivating disdain and social turmoil. As we wrestle with the repercussions of a worldwide pandemic, the separation points of our cultural designs are revealed, uncovering the weaknesses that request quick consideration and review.

Schooling, long proclaimed as the extraordinary balancer, winds up at a junction. The computerized partition worsens existing differences, as admittance to quality instruction turns into an honor instead of a right. The divergence in instructive open doors reverberations into financial imbalance, restricting vertical portability and sustaining a pattern of neediness. The source of inspiration requests a reconsideration of our obligation to instruction as a crucial common liberty, open to all, regardless of financial status or geological area.

In addition, the source of inspiration resounds inside the passages of force, rocking the boat of political frameworks that time after time focus on momentary additions over long haul supportability. The nexus between corporate interests and political independent direction has caused a culture of smugness, thwarting advancement on basic issues. As we explore the intricate landscape of worldwide administration, the call entices pioneers to rise above the bounds of sectarian governmental issues and embrace a dream that focuses on the benefit of all, cultivating global participation and cooperation.

The computerized age, with its commitment of network and data, likewise carries with it new difficulties to individual protection and independence. The source of inspiration reverberations in the discussion encompassing information morals, asking social orders to lay out strong structures that protect the privileges of people in an undeniably interconnected world. The approach of computerized reasoning and mechanization brings up significant issues about the fate of work and the dissemination of abundance. The call requests a proactive way to deal with explore the moral situations presented by these mechanical headways, guaranteeing that progress doesn't come at the expense of human nobility.

In the midst of these difficulties, the source of inspiration tracks down motivation in the versatility of networks that meet up notwithstanding misfortune. Grassroots developments, driven by the energy and responsibility of people, have the ability to impact groundbreaking change. The call supports the sustaining of a culture that enables people to become influencers inside their networks, encouraging a feeling of obligation and responsibility that rises above geographic limits.

The direness of the source of inspiration is highlighted by the approaching phantom of a worldwide wellbeing emergency. The Coronavirus pandemic, an unmistakable sign of the interconnectedness of our reality, has uncovered the delicacy of our wellbeing frameworks and the deficiencies of our readiness. As we wrestle with the quick difficulties of the pandemic, the call reverberates in the basic to fabricate versatile wellbeing frameworks that focus on avoidance, value, and openness. A call perceives the indivisible connection between individual wellbeing and the strength of the worldwide local area.

The source of inspiration stretches out its range to the domain of social protection, recognizing the lavishness of variety as a foundation of human civilization. In a period where social legacy is compromised by globalization and homogenization, the call encourages a purposeful work to protect and praise the heap articulations of human imagination. It is a call to connect the holes between societies, encouraging common comprehension and regard that rises above semantic, strict, and ethnic partitions.

At its center, the source of inspiration is a request to rediscover our common mankind. In a world divided by philosophical contrasts and international strains, the call reverberations in the requirement for sympathy and empathy. It provokes people to look past their nearby worries and perceive the interconnectedness of all life on this planet. A call rises above borders, welcoming cooperation and fortitude despite shared difficulties.

The pathway to noting this call isn't without deterrents. It requires a crucial change in outlook, a takeoff from the latency of carelessness, and a promise to the difficult work of change. It requests that people, networks, and countries put making peace at the forefront and work cooperatively toward shared objectives.

It requires a rethinking of our frameworks and foundations, mixing them with a feeling of direction that heads past the quest for individual increase.

Schooling arises as a key part in the acknowledgment of this extraordinary vision. A reenvisioned schooling system turns into the cauldron for sustaining decisive reasoning, inventiveness, and a feeling of worldwide citizenship. It is a call to instructors to rise above the constraints of conventional instructional method, embracing inventive methodologies that outfit understudies with the abilities and information expected to explore the intricacies of the cutting edge world. It is a call to understudies to become dynamic members in their own learning, to address suppositions, and to develop a feeling of obligation toward the more extensive local area.

Similarly significant is the job of organizations and partnerships in noticing the source of inspiration. The business scene isn't excluded from the basic for change. A change in outlook is required, one that perceives the cooperative connection between corporate achievement and cultural prosperity. The call moves organizations to embrace economical practices, to focus on moral contemplations in direction, and to contribute seriously to the networks where they work. It is a call to move past a thin spotlight on overall revenues and embrace a comprehensive comprehension of progress that envelops ecological stewardship, social obligation, and moral initiative.

Inside the domain of legislative issues, the source of inspiration requires a recalibration of needs. It requests that pioneers focus on the drawn out interests of their constituents over transient additions. It is a call to rise above the nearsightedness of hardliner legislative issues and fashion a way toward strategies that address the underlying drivers of cultural difficulties. The call resounds in the basic to assemble comprehensive administration structures that enhance the voices of the underestimated and guarantee that dynamic cycles are straightforward, responsible, and participatory.

The source of inspiration isn't bound to the domain of strategy and administration; it stretches out into the ordinary decisions and activities of people. It provokes every individual to think about their utilization designs, to think about the natural and social effect of their decisions. It is a call to embrace a more maintainable and cognizant approach to everyday life, perceiving the interconnectedness of individual activities with the more extensive texture of the worldwide local area. It is a call to develop a mentality of stewardship, where people see themselves not as latent purchasers but rather as dynamic supporters of the prosperity of the planet and its occupants.

The source of inspiration likewise reverberates in the domain of global relations, where the basic for coordinated effort and collaboration is more squeezing than any other time in recent memory. Worldwide difficulties, be they environmental change, pandemics, or monetary emergencies, rise above public boundaries.

The call coaxes countries to move past limited personal responsibility and embrace a feeling of fortitude. It is a call to encourage political connections in light of shared regard, discourse, and a common obligation to tending to the normal difficulties confronting humankind.

Notwithstanding this source of inspiration, idleness and opposition are extravagances that mankind can sick manage. The results of inaction are too desperate, the stakes excessively high. The call requests a takeoff from the recognizable, a readiness to wander into an unfamiliar area in quest for a superior future. It requires versatility despite difficulty, an acknowledgment that the excursion toward positive change will be laden with difficulties and mishaps.

A call recognizes the innate force of the person to impact change, to be an impetus for a more extensive change. It perceives that every individual, no matter what their experience or situation, has office and impact. It is a call to tackle that office, to channel individual endeavors into an aggregate power for good. A call scatters the legend of feebleness, reminding people that their decisions, regardless of how little, add to the molding of the world.

9.1 The path forward: responsible nanotechnology development

The direction of innovative progression has, since forever ago, formed the course of human development. In the 21st hundred years, the union of different logical disciplines has led to nanotechnology — a field with the possibility to reform ventures, medication, and day to day existence. As we stand at the edge of extraordinary potential outcomes, the basic to direct the improvement of nanotechnology with obligation and prescience becomes central. The way ahead should be one of cautious thought, moral reflection, and a promise to outfit the force of nanotechnology to improve humankind while limiting expected gambles.

Nanotechnology, extensively characterized as the control of issue at the nanoscale, includes working with materials and designs at the sub-atomic and nuclear levels. This degree of accuracy offers a scope of chances, from improving the proficiency of energy creation to reforming clinical diagnostics and treatment. Be that as it may, likewise with any useful asset, the capable improvement of nanotechnology requires a nuanced comprehension of its suggestions and a proactive way to deal with address moral, social, and ecological worries.

One of the essential moral contemplations in nanotechnology advancement spins around the possible effect on human wellbeing. The capacity to design materials at the nanoscale brings up issues about the wellbeing of nanoparticles and their associations with living creatures. While nanotechnology holds guarantee for imaginative medication conveyance frameworks and designated treatments, there is a requirement for thorough examination to survey the drawn out impacts of openness to nanoparticles on human wellbeing. The preparatory standard ought to direct the improvement of nanomaterials, inciting specialists and enterprises with focus on security evaluations and comply to moral rules.

Past wellbeing contemplations, the moral components of nanotechnology stretch out to issues of protection, security, and cultural ramifications. The combination of nanoscale sensors and gadgets into regular items presents the possibility of universal reconnaissance and information assortment. Mindful advancement involves laying out powerful moral structures to safeguard individual protection, guaranteeing that the advantages of nanotechnology are not offset by the disintegration of individual flexibilities. Furthermore, the potential for noxious purposes of nanotechnology, for example, the advancement of nanomaterials for destructive purposes, highlights the requirement for worldwide participation in laying out moral principles and administrative systems to forestall abuse.

Natural supportability is one more basic aspect of capable nanotechnology improvement. The creation and removal of nanomaterials may have biological results that require cautious thought. Specialists and enterprises should focus on the advancement of harmless to the ecosystem nanomaterials and processes, limiting the biological impression related with nanotechnology applications. Life cycle evaluations and complete examinations on the ecological effect of nanomaterials ought to be indispensable parts of dependable advancement works on, directing leaders toward practical decisions.

As nanotechnology propels, the moral ramifications of controlling living life forms at the sub-atomic level come to the cutting edge. The area of nanobiotechnology, which investigates the point of interaction among nanotechnology and science, holds massive commitment for clinical leap forwards, like designated drug conveyance and customized medication. Nonetheless, moral quandaries emerge while considering the potential for human improvement through nanotechnological intercessions. Mindful improvement requests a smart assessment of the moral limits encompassing human increase, with an accentuation on guaranteeing that the advantages are impartially circulated and that the potential for fueling existing social disparities is relieved.

In the domain of nanoelectronics and figuring, the quest for ever-more modest and all the more impressive gadgets raises worries about the ecological effect of electronic waste. Capable nanotechnology improvement requires a guarantee to planning electronic parts in view of reusing and maintainability. Specialists and enterprises should investigate novel materials and manufacture methods that limit the ecological impression of electronic gadgets. Moreover, the mindful removal and reusing of nanoelectronic parts ought to be vital to the existence cycle the executives of these advancements.

An area of developing worry in the improvement of nanotechnology is the potential for international strains and security chances. As countries strive for authority in mechanical advancement, the competition to foster high level nanotechnologies might uplift international rivalry. Capable improvement requires global joint effort and the foundation of clear standards and conventions to forestall the weaponization of nanotechnology and relieve the gamble of another weapons contest.

Moral contemplations should direct policymakers in offsetting public safety interests with the aggregate liability to guarantee the protected and gainful advancement of nanotechnology for all of humankind.

The way ahead in dependable nanotechnology improvement likewise requests a comprehensive methodology that thinks about the points of view and needs of assorted partners. Drawing in with the general population, policymakers, ethicists, and delegates from underestimated networks is significant to forming a future where the advantages of nanotechnology are impartially conveyed. Open discourse and straightforward correspondence about the dangers and advantages of nanotechnology encourage a feeling of shared liability and engage people to partake in dynamic cycles that shape the direction of mechanical turn of events.

In the instructive circle, capable nanotechnology advancement requires an accentuation on cultivating moral mindfulness and decisive reasoning among future researchers, architects, and policymakers. Coordinating morals instruction into educational plans guarantees that those at the front line of nanotechnology exploration and application are outfitted with the moral structures important to explore complex moral difficulties. Moral proficiency turns into a fundamental apparatus in the tool stash of experts working in nanotechnology-related fields, directing them toward capable navigation and guaranteeing that moral contemplations are essential to the improvement cycle.

The cooperation between the scholarly community, industry, and government is urgent in laying out the underpinnings of mindful nanotechnology improvement. Hearty administrative systems, informed by interdisciplinary ability, are fundamental for guide the protected and moral improvement of nanotechnologies. Policymakers should work pair with researchers, ethicists, and industry pioneers to make regulation that tends to the one of a kind difficulties presented by nanotechnology while encouraging development. An equilibrium should be struck between empowering progress and shielding against expected chances, with a pledge to adjusting guidelines as the field develops.

Industry pioneers assume a vital part in establishing the vibe for dependable nanotechnology improvement. Moral strategic approaches, straightforwardness in innovative work, and a promise to manageability should be at the front of corporate systems. Industry affiliations can work with the foundation of moral rules and best works on, encouraging a culture of liability that reaches out across the nanotechnology area. By focusing on moral contemplations in direction, industry pioneers can add to building public trust and trust in the advantages of nanotechnology.

Worldwide coordinated effort is essential in tending to the worldwide difficulties presented by nanotechnology advancement. The interconnected idea of the world requests that countries cooperate to lay out normal guidelines, share information, and direction endeavors to guarantee the dependable advancement of nanotechnologies.

Worldwide associations, like the Unified Countries and its particular organizations, can give a stage to exchange, participation, and the improvement of worldwide standards that guide the moral and safe utilization of nanotechnology on a worldwide scale.

The way ahead in mindful nanotechnology advancement is one that requires persistent reflection, transformation, and cooperation. As the field develops, so too should our moral structures, administrative components, and instructive methodologies. The difficulties and open doors introduced by nanotechnology are dynamic, and dependable improvement requires a continuous obligation to remaining at the cutting edge of moral contemplations and cultural ramifications.

9.2 Ensuring the benefits of nanotechnology while minimizing risks

The approach of nanotechnology, with its phenomenal capacity to control matter at the sub-atomic and nuclear levels, holds monstrous commitment for changing different aspects of human existence. From medication to energy, nanotechnology can possibly alter enterprises and address squeezing worldwide difficulties. Nonetheless, the acknowledgment of these advantages is joined by moral, ecological, and social dangers that request cautious thought. Guaranteeing the capable improvement of nanotechnology requires an exhaustive methodology that expands the possible advantages as well as limits expected gambles, cultivating an equilibrium that focuses on the prosperity of humankind and the climate.

At the front line of moral contemplations in nanotechnology is the possible effect on human wellbeing. The control of materials at the nanoscale presents novel properties that might associate with organic frameworks in unanticipated ways. As nanomaterials find applications in medication, for example, in drug conveyance frameworks and demonstrative devices, the requirement for thorough security appraisals becomes vital. Long haul openness to nanoparticles and their likely aggregation in organs raise worries about harmfulness and unanticipated wellbeing impacts. Dependable improvement requires broad examination into the organic cooperations of nanomaterials, with an emphasis on figuring out their expected dangers and advantages.

Notwithstanding wellbeing contemplations, the moral ramifications of nanotechnology reach out to issues of protection and security. The reconciliation of nanoscale sensors into regular items, shaping the Web of Things (IoT), raises worries about pervasive reconnaissance and the assortment of individual information. The capable advancement of nanotechnology requires the foundation of hearty moral structures to protect individual security. Finding some kind of harmony between the comfort presented by IoT gadgets and the insurance of individual data is fundamental to guarantee that the advantages of nanotechnology don't come to the detriment of individual opportunities.

Additionally, the potential for pernicious purposes of nanotechnology presents security gambles with that should be tended to. The improvement of nanomaterials for hurtful purposes, for example, in the production of cutting edge weaponry, highlights the requirement for worldwide participation in laying out moral principles and administrative systems. Capable administration should be proactive in expecting and moderating security chances related with nanotechnology, forestalling its weaponization and guaranteeing that the innovation is bridled for tranquil and valuable purposes.

Natural maintainability is a basic part of mindful nanotechnology improvement. The creation, use, and removal of nanomaterials may have biological results that need cautious thought. Life cycle evaluations and complete examinations on the natural effect of nanomaterials ought to be necessary parts of capable advancement rehearses. Endeavors to plan harmless to the ecosystem nanomaterials and processes, as well as methodologies for the dependable removal of nanoproducts, add to limiting the natural impression related with nanotechnology applications.

As nanotechnology propels, moral situations emerge in the domain of human upgrade. The intermingling of nanotechnology with biotechnology raises the possibility of increasing human abilities, from mental upgrades to actual adjustments. Mindful improvement requires cautious thought of the moral limits encompassing human increase, with an emphasis on guaranteeing that any upgrades are protected, open, and don't compound existing social imbalances. Moral rules should be laid out to explore the intricate landscape of human upgrade, finding some kind of harmony between the possible advantages and the moral ramifications of changing the human condition at the nanoscale.

In the field of nanoelectronics and registering, the quest for more modest and all the more remarkable gadgets raises worries about electronic waste and asset consumption. Capable nanotechnology improvement requests a guarantee to planning electronic parts in light of reusing and manageability. Analysts and businesses should investigate materials and creation procedures that limit the ecological effect of electronic gadgets. Moreover, capable removal and reusing practices ought to be vital to the existence cycle the executives of nanoelectronic parts, forestalling the gathering of electronic waste and its related natural dangers.

The dependable improvement of nanotechnology requires a comprehensive methodology that thinks about the viewpoints and necessities of assorted partners. Drawing in with people in general, policymakers, ethicists, and delegates from underestimated networks is vital for molding a future where the advantages of nanotechnology are impartially disseminated. Open discourse and straightforward correspondence about the dangers and advantages of nanotechnology encourage a feeling of shared liability and engage people to partake in dynamic cycles that shape the direction of mechanical turn of events.

Schooling assumes a critical part in guaranteeing mindful nanotechnology improvement. Cultivating moral mindfulness and decisive reasoning among researchers, specialists, policymakers, and the overall population is fundamental. Coordinating morals schooling into educational programs guarantees that those engaged with nanotechnology exploration and application are furnished with the moral structures important to explore complex moral issues. Moral education turns into a fundamental apparatus for experts working in nanotechnology-related fields, directing them toward mindful navigation and guaranteeing that moral contemplations are basic to the improvement cycle.

The coordinated effort between the scholarly community, industry, and government is critical in laying out the groundworks of dependable nanotechnology advancement. Vigorous administrative systems, informed by interdisciplinary mastery, are crucial for guide the protected and moral improvement of nanotechnologies. Policymakers should work pair with researchers, ethicists, and industry pioneers to create regulation that tends to the extraordinary difficulties presented by nanotechnology while encouraging advancement. An equilibrium should be struck between empowering progress and shielding against likely dangers, with a promise to adjusting guidelines as the field develops.

Industry pioneers assume a urgent part in establishing the vibe for capable nanotechnology improvement. Moral strategic policies, straightforwardness in innovative work, and a guarantee to supportability should be at the very front of corporate techniques. Industry affiliations can work with the foundation of moral rules and best works on, cultivating a culture of liability that reaches out across the nanotechnology area. By focusing on moral contemplations in direction, industry pioneers can add to building public trust and trust in the advantages of nanotechnology.

Worldwide cooperation is crucial in tending to the worldwide difficulties presented by nanotechnology advancement. The interconnected idea of the world requests that countries cooperate to lay out normal principles, share information, and direction endeavors to guarantee the mindful advancement of nanotechnologies. Worldwide associations, like the Unified Countries and its particular organizations, can give a stage to discourse, participation, and the improvement of worldwide standards that guide the moral and safe utilization of nanotechnology on a worldwide scale.

The way ahead in guaranteeing the advantages of nanotechnology while limiting dangers is one that requires nonstop reflection, variation, and coordinated effort. As the field develops, so too should our moral structures, administrative systems, and instructive methodologies. The difficulties and amazing open doors introduced by nanotechnology are dynamic, and guaranteeing capable improvement requires a continuous obligation to remaining at the cutting edge of moral contemplations and cultural ramifications.

9.3 The need for public engagement, ethical considerations, and sustainable innovation

In the quickly propelling scene of mechanical advancement, the requirement for public commitment, moral contemplations, and feasible practices has never been more articulated. As society remains on the cliff of pivotal progressions, especially in fields like man-made brainpower, biotechnology, and environmentally friendly power, it is basic to perceive the multi-layered influence these advancements might have on people, networks, and the planet. Public commitment, moral systems, and manageability contemplations are basic parts in guiding the direction of development towards a future that isn't just mechanically progressed yet in addition socially capable and naturally reasonable.

Public commitment fills in as a foundation in forming the heading of mechanical development. In a period set apart by exceptional network and admittance to data, including the general population in the dynamic cycles encompassing mechanical headways is both a vote based basic and a commonsense need. Public commitment goes past simple data spread; it involves dynamic cooperation, conference, and coordinated effort with different partners, including local area individuals, support gatherings, and people straightforwardly impacted by innovative turns of events.

A basic part of public commitment is guaranteeing that the advantages and dangers of mechanical developments are conveyed straightforwardly. The intricacy of arising innovations, like quality altering or high level man-made reasoning, requires a continuous discourse between researchers, policymakers, and people in general. Straightforward correspondence cultivates a superior comprehension of the likely ramifications of these innovations, permitting people to go with informed choices and add to the forming of moral rules and administrative structures.

Moral contemplations structure the ethical compass that directs the capable turn of events and organization of arising innovations. The moral components of development become especially articulated while managing issues like hereditary designing, security concerns connected with man-made brainpower, or the utilization of cutting edge innovations in reconnaissance. Laying out moral systems requires a comprehensive assessment of the expected effects on people, networks, and more extensive society, guaranteeing that the quest for development lines up with central qualities like independence, equity, and the insurance of common liberties.

One of the critical moral contemplations in mechanical advancement spins around the potential for unseen side-effects. The advancement of new innovations frequently dominates our capacity to expect and address moral difficulties. Consequently, a proactive methodology that incorporates moral contemplations into the beginning phases of innovative work is urgent. Moral effect appraisals, closely resembling natural effect evaluations, can help recognize and alleviate expected moral worries before advancements are broadly sent.

Also, the moral ramifications of mechanical advancement reach out to issues of value and civil rights. The alleged "computerized partition" embodies the variations in admittance to innovation, where certain populaces, frequently minimized or monetarily burdened, need the assets and chances to partake in the advantages of mechanical progressions completely. Moral contemplations request a guarantee to restricting these holes, guaranteeing that the advantages of development are open to all and don't fuel existing social imbalances.

The idea of capable advancement stresses a moral methodology that goes past simple consistence with guidelines. Capable development requires a guarantee to moral standards, maintainability, and a consistent discourse with partners. It involves expecting and tending to moral difficulties all through the advancement lifecycle, from the conceptualization of thoughts to the scattering of innovations in the public arena. This approach cultivates a culture of responsibility and moral care among trailblazers, empowering them to think about the more extensive cultural ramifications of their work.

Maintainability contemplations are indispensable to the dependable improvement of innovation. As the worldwide local area wrestles with the difficulties of environmental change, asset consumption, and ecological corruption, advancement should be lined up with the standards of maintainability. This involves not just limiting the ecological effect of mechanical cycles yet additionally creating arrangements that contribute decidedly to natural preservation and recovery.

The progress to a maintainable future requires a change in perspective in the manner development is conceptualized and carried out. Maintainable advancement includes the improvement of innovations that address squeezing natural difficulties, like clean energy arrangements, effective waste administration frameworks, and feasible farming practices. It likewise includes a reconsideration of utilization designs, empowering the improvement of innovations that advance round economies, asset productivity, and decreased ecological impression.

Environmentally friendly power advancements represent the crossing point of development, morals, and maintainability. The turn of events and far and wide reception of environmentally friendly power sources, for example, sun oriented and wind power, address a huge move toward relieving the ecological effect of energy creation. Moral contemplations in this setting envelop issues like the fair appropriation of advantages, the simply change for networks impacted by the shift away from conventional energy sources, and the capable administration of electronic waste produced by environmentally friendly power advancements.

In the domain of biotechnology, moral and manageability contemplations combine in conversations about hereditary designing, quality altering, and manufactured science. The capacity to control the hereditary code of living organic entities brings up significant moral issues about the expected ramifications for biodiversity, natural frameworks, and the ethical ramifications of changing the central structure blocks of life.

Supportability contemplations in biotechnology include dependable stewardship of hereditary assets, guaranteeing that advancement in this field lines up with standards of environmental honesty and the safeguarding of biodiversity.

The idea of "manageable turn of events" underscores an all encompassing methodology that adjusts monetary, social, and natural aspects. Mechanical advancement, when directed by the standards of supportable turn of events, turns into a power for positive change. This requires a shift away from a thin spotlight on momentary gains and benefit expansion toward a more far reaching comprehension of development as an instrument for tending to worldwide difficulties and further developing the prosperity of present and people in the future.

Public commitment, moral contemplations, and supportability are interconnected components that aggregately add to the dependable and comprehensive advancement of innovation. In drawing in the general population, there is an affirmation of the assorted points of view and values that mold society. Moral contemplations give an ethical structure that guarantees the mindful utilization of innovation in arrangement with cultural qualities. Maintainability contemplations guide development toward arrangements that address present issues as well as protect the prosperity of people in the future and the planet.

A valid example is the improvement of shrewd urban areas, where the incorporation of innovation into metropolitan foundation plans to upgrade productivity, network, and personal satisfaction. Public commitment becomes fundamental in the preparation and execution of shrewd city drives, guaranteeing that the different necessities and inclinations of the local area are considered. Moral contemplations envelop issues like protection in the time of omnipresent sensors and information assortment, as well as inquiries regarding the evenhanded conveyance of advantages and possible adverse consequences on weak populaces. Practical development in brilliant urban communities includes planning metropolitan frameworks that limit asset utilization, diminish discharges, and upgrade versatility to the effects of environmental change.